Entertaining at Home with Ease

Entertaining
at Home
with
Ease

Jean Amis Baugh
and
Marjorie S. Stewart

To my friend with love,

Jean A. Baugh

Marjorie S. Stewart
Luke 10:38-42

BROADMAN PRESS
Nashville, Tennessee

© Copyright 1988 • Broadman Press
All rights reserved
4270-04
ISBN: 0-8054-7004-2

Dewey Decimal Classification: 642
Subject Heading: ENTERTAINING
Library of Congress Catalog Card Number: 87-21809

Printed in the United States of America

Unless otherwise noted, all Scripture quotations are taken from the King James Version. Scripture quotations marked TLB are taken from *The Living Bible.* Copyright © Tyndale House Publishers, Wheaton, Illinois, 1971. Used by permission.

Library of Congress Cataloging-in-Publication Data

Baugh, Jean Amis, 1927-
  Entertaining at home with ease.

  1. Entertaining.   I. Stewart, Marjorie S.,
1927-   . II. Title.
TX731.B365   1988   642'.4   87-21809
ISBN 0-8054-7004-2

To Frank and Bill

Husbands helpful beyond belief
with whom we have shared it all.

Contents

Entertaining at Home with Ease

1
No One's Cooking Anymore

If you have any interest in being hospitable and able to entertain more easily, this book is written for you.

Our purpose in this book is to share what we have learned about entertaining—how to manage so it is possible and enjoyable. That includes financially, for certainly we all have limitations; emotionally, so we do not become stressed if every occasion is not candlelight and roses; and with economy of time so as not to be deprived of entertaining for months on end.

As Christians, we are honestly amazed by how often the Scriptures mention food. One treasured account tells that He who had nowhere to lay His head was the thoughtful host who prepared an early morning breakfast by the Sea of Galilee. Jesus even invited the disciples to bring some of their catch. What a lovely invitation: "Come and dine" (John 21:9-12)!

Is something missing in our homes today? Is our life-style so chaotic that finding time for enjoying guests in our homes is a thing of the past? Are we and our friends limited to what we can share in a restaurant or theater or park? Can we never say, "Come to our home and share this part of our lives"?

Surely in His will, there is a way for Christians to share

their blessings, and these certainly include our homes and families. If our lives are so busy we can never enjoy the fellowship of others, perhaps we should check and make sure that what we are doing is worth the price.

You may ask why the two of us feel we have insights to write a book to make it easier for you to entertain. Have our experiences been any different from any other working homemaker? Some have been unique, but in another sense they haven't, for life's experiences are fairly common to all. In any case, we offer you what we have learned.

Jean has spent thirty-six years with the same guy, rearing their three children on three continents. Food has been really enjoyed, whether eaten with fingers from a banana leaf, with chopsticks from a melon rind, or with stainless cutlery in a country where sterling would have been turned into bangles, one piece at a time, if we had taken it there.

While we (Baughs) served as missionaries in Bangladesh and in Tanzania, East Africa, entertaining and being entertained ran the gambit of extremes. We have been the honored guests of Bengali refugees at the only meal of the year when they were able to have meat. In contrast, we have dined in elegance with the Aga Khan. We have entertained a Masai woman who had never been inside a house or eaten a bite in the presence of her husband. That was the same week the American ambassador and his entourage came to lunch!

In both Bangladesh and Tanzania, our home was two days of travel time from a city with adequate hotel accommodations. Often we had drop-in as well as planned guests, sometimes for weeks at a time. It was usually unwise to tell guests exactly what they were eating. Never did they fail to comment on how delicious the food was. Homemade (warthog) sausage, (goat) curry, mushrooms cut from the front yard, (zebra) burgers, made-from-scratch everything, locally grown and home-roasted coffee, and candied-from-fresh-pineapples in fruitcakes can be wonderful fare.

The overseas communities in East Africa and Bangladesh taught me much about being hospitable. No traveler ever leaves a home without food and clean water for the journey, for towns may be a day's travel apart. Tea times in overseas British homes are 10:00 AM and 4:00 PM. Any friend can expect refreshments just by stopping in at those hours. The Bengali people of Bangladesh would not think of letting you stop by without offering you the very best they have, even when it is their only food.

Often I have entertained someone like my old friend Mama Vassa, an ancient little Hindu woman. We had no common spoken language but loved each other dearly and delighted in finding ways to show it. We smiled, we hugged, and we enjoyed giving gifts to each other; we cooked delicacies for each other; we shared our faiths the best we could; and we cried when we parted.

Today, as an extension home economist, I no longer have that kind of time. Unless I find a way to develop and cherish friends, I shall miss a very precious part of living. "Entertaining" necessarily becomes less and less elaborate and more sharing a meal, enjoying each other over a freezer of ice cream, or picking up an entrée at a carry-out restaurant on the way home from work. Either way, the purpose is accomplished if relationships are enhanced.

I was struck by the contrast in the changing American style of hospitality during one furlough back in the United States. About halfway through our leave, a realization hit me. While our family and friends had been most gracious in the welcome we received, all but a few of them had entertained us in beautiful restaurants or clubs. It seemed that no one was cooking anymore.

When I mentioned this to Marge, my longtime friend, she expressed surprise. She had experienced the same thing, but had credited it to the fact that her professional background might intimidate some.

So both of us began to understand the great change occurring. The thought of entertaining after a forty-hour work week in addition to homemaking chores was more than most women could face.

As co-author, Marge has had a life-style many career women may recognize as their own. We could best describe it as the great American balancing act. It consists in driving toward personal excellence both at home and in our professions. As Marge says, some would say I've reached the top, but I've been at the bottom, too.

I've had forty-one years with a husband who has been more supportive than most men. When our son started to kindergarten, my husband encouraged me to start to college.

Then, without realizing just what was happening, I found myself on a treadmill that never stopped, beginning with a B.S. from UCLA and ten years later received a Ph.D. from the Ohio State University. In addition to varied career changes and homemaking roles, the last eleven years I have spent as dean of a college of home economics.

Food has always been an important part of our lives. When our son was home, he often helped with kitchen chores; and my husband, in spite of his own demanding schedule, has always shared in the shopping, preparation, and serving of food for both ourselves and our guests. Thus our family has been a team. I couldn't have survived without them.

Our entertaining has varied from providing a large noon meal for harvest hands to having sit-down dinners for top university administrators. In between, there were plenty of fun meals and parties for friends and family. Most of all, we have enjoyed the times when we have entertained two or more friends at a simple meal followed by a quiet evening together.

As a result of health problems, it has been necessary for me to retire early, and consequently we are limiting our entertaining to more simple styles. But the world over, food and fellowship is the ultimate of hospitality. There is no greater compliment that you can pay anyone than to invite that person to your home to share even simple fare. It hasn't always been easy to learn that humble fact.

The many practical suggestions which follow are simply the result of the combined years of our experiences and those of others . . . our families and friends.

JEAN BAUGH AND MARJORIE STEWART

2
A Matter of Motivation

In searching Scripture for what it teaches concerning entertaining or being hospitable, we find many examples. Beginning in Genesis where Abraham warmly welcomed three strangers and going all the way through the New Testament, there are illustrations of meeting the physical and social needs of strangers as well as loved ones. Stories are told of friendships which could have developed only through many hours of sharing and caring.

The writer of Proverbs wisely observed that a person who wants friends must show himself to be "friendly" (Prov. 18:24). This is easily accepted, but it's harder to accept Jesus' admonition to the leaders of the Pharisees to invite to their meals those who couldn't reciprocate—the poor, the maimed, the lame, and the blind. We are forced to remember His words: As much as you do it "unto one of the least of these my brethren," you do it unto me (Matt. 25:40).

But we see that Jesus did not limit hospitality to those who were less fortunate, for while He fed the masses, He also fed His own. Another truth comes to light in this example. Remember when He fed the five thousand? He let His disciples be a part of the miracle. They not only witnessed this wondrous provision, but they also were instruments in the blessing! His power is not diminished, and He wants to work through us today.

Jesus treasured His friends. His visits with Mary, Martha, and Lazarus reveal an intimacy which could only be born of much time spent together. They ministered to each other's needs in turn. He withdrew to the refuge of their loving home, and each of them was blessed because of it. Think of Mary's new understanding as she absorbed every word Jesus spoke.

It was as if the words had a life of their own. Among His teachings He held that when believers entertained strangers or fed and clothed people who needed it or visited the sick, it was the same as doing it for God. No wonder she had felt—well, almost exalted—when she'd drawn water to give a thirsty traveler a cool drink!

Savoring the new revelation that God wanted to use people to do ordinary things in His name, Mary lost all consciousness of time and responsibility. Her heart was singing paeons of praise that God had a place for her in His good plan. She didn't have to be a rabbi or a priest to serve her God. As a woman, she could never hope to do those jobs anyway. But these hospitable things she and Martha were always doing in love for others were a gift to the Almighty Jehovah Himself! This she could do and rejoice in doing it. Mary's heart overflowed with joy and thanksgiving.

The more pragmatic Martha at that point was not on a spiritual high, however, and Jesus had to calm her when she exploded that day in Bethany. Most of us would be just like Martha—overdoing, worrying about the details, and emphasizing the physical over the spiritual. Can we learn from this very typical event where to put our priorities?

It thrills us to remember that after the resurrection, Jesus prepared breakfast by the Sea of Galilee for the weary disci-

ples who had fished all night without success. He was minis-
tering to their hurting hearts as much as to their physical
hunger. But the best is yet to come. Someday He will celebrate with us the marriage supper of the Lamb! It is too
much for our finite minds to comprehend.

Progressing past the Gospels in Scripture to where the
writers instruct believers, we are told in Romans to be "giv-
en to hospitality" (12:13), in Hebrews to "be not forgetful
to entertain strangers" (13:2), in 1 Peter to "use hospitality
one to another without grudging" (4:9), and in Titus to be
"a lover of hospitality" (1:8).

Being hospitable or reaching out to others begins in the
heart. We love, and thus we want to share. In almost every
culture, eating together is symbolic of peace, acceptance,
and friendship. Lasting relationships are built around the
table. Even young children learn some of their most valu-
able lifetime lessons around the family table and in sharing
food with others. Caring is born at home.

Some of us entertain in our homes partly to ensure our
insulation from loneliness. This is especially true if we live
in a large town or city. Our work associates, church friends,
neighbors, club members, and others may be interesting
people, but often we interact with them on a superficial
level. Most of us long for a few close friends with whom we
can relax and feel secure and who know us as we are but
love us anyway.

The more impersonal and "high tech" this society
becomes, the more we need these treasured close relationships. Nurturing special bonds takes a lot of self-investment
in time, energy, and money.

Our husbands say it in a very practical way: we entertain
either because we want to or because we have to. Perhaps,

but usually we choose to without even recognizing all that motivates us.

Many times the motivation for entertaining is counterfeit, such as the woman who bought all new bedspreads the day before her big party and then returned them all to the store the following day. Impressing guests with material possessions should be outside the realm of born-again believers. It is essential that we be willing to reveal ourselves as we actually are, worn carpet and all, before we can achieve an honest, open relationship with another. As that makes us vulnerable to the other person, it is something that we do gradually over time as we learn to trust. With understanding, caring and compassion grow.

There doesn't have to be a high and lofty motive for being hospitable. It is great just to ask friends over for no reason. Or we may want them to share some joy or see a finished project. Perhaps spur-of-the-moment times are the best. We remember a cold night when one of us called the other couple to share in lighting the Christmas candles and to have refreshments. Moments like these are especially sweet because there are many rushed parties, laden with marvelous morsels, and far too few truly relaxing moments during any holiday season.

Not that the festive times aren't important. They are and should be. We know from the Bible and from studying history how important the Feast Days, weddings, and other times were in the lives of the Jews. The days were filled with emotion, tradition, and memories. Christians also have Christmas, Easter, and intimate family times to draw family and friends together and to God.

Days of remembrance are indelible times. Research shows that successful people have grown up in homes with significant traditions. Our mobile society is making this

more difficult, and thus we need to work even more dili-
gently to make these notable traditional days a part of our
lives.

But what about the other days and evenings of our lives?
We don't live in isolation or in a vacuum: Can that same
spirit which sparked Abraham compel us to touch others'
lives by being hospitable? Can we cope with entertaining
as an occasional reality?

We certainly don't want to impose a guilt trip on ourselves or anyone else. Some passages in our lives are such
that we simply can't handle guests or even family. An illness
or unusual stress may dictate that entertaining should be
kept to a minimum. Seclusion may be in order. But time
does heal many problems, and our circumstances do
change. As social beings we then need to rise from our
self-imposed exile to a fresh new start.

While we do want to be servants of the Lord, it's OK to
have secular reasons for entertaining. Family members who
want to help others advance in their careers have a logical
motivation to be hospitable. A gracious, capable, and truly
hospitable family is an asset to any organization.

If we tried to list all the reasons we want to entertain, we
would never have time to do it. Any reason is sufficient. The
employed homemaker must use more discretion simply because her time and energy are more limited. Whether it is
an occasion for rejoicing, certain people to get to know, or
a need to be met, making people welcome in your life is a
gift to cultivate and to enjoy.

However, graciousness is not limited to sharing joys.
Sometimes we need to be together to comfort one another.
This may involve taking food to someone following the
death of a family member or showing other personal concerns at those tender moments, but it is a gift of love. Jean

has volunteered for kitchen duty in a home during the critical hours. Wouldn't that be welcome? Marge has taken a sack of disposable kitchen helpers (napkins, cups, plates) plus staples such as milk, coffee, or soft drinks to complement the casseroles, hams, and pastries brought in by thoughtful neighbors. Hospitality isn't bound by our own four walls. The opportunities are infinite.

A single friend said to us, "I don't know anyone to invite home from church." We suggested that she consider another single lady, a senior citizen, a church staff member, a handicapped person, a university student, someone unemployed, or newcomers to the church or the neighborhood. And we asked if there weren't some business or professional acquaintances she might ask over for a Sunday lunch. Even a meal primarily supplied from the deli can be fun when shared.

Most people are not starving for food as much as they are hungry for the human touch. Usually, this type of fellowship seems more mellow in the environment of our home—whether it is a small apartment, a home shared with another, the vacation getaway, a mansion, or a modest home.

Some of our most precious memories with other couples have been last-minute invitations after evening church for popcorn and cold drinks or homemade ice cream. Or there was the time that Jean and her family dedicated their new, unfinished home while seated on the plastic-covered carpet in the dining room, surrounded by candlelight and boxes of chicken from a fast-food restaurant. Lifetime relationships have been sealed in such simple settings.

Both of us have opened our homes and shared them with someone just needing a refuge for the night or longer. Sometimes it involved caring for the aches of their human bruises. But mostly, it just included furnishing a convenient place to stay when there was nothing else near or within guests' pocketbooks. Regardless, we were trying to show that we are Christians by our love and our willingness to be inconvenienced to demonstrate that love. However, for many of us, our first priority is to stay in touch with the people we care about and to strengthen the relationships that bind us by including them in our private worlds—our homes.

If you are serious about entertaining, don't get all hung up by the obligatory entertaining you feel due someone from your past experiences. Get the obligations taken care of with specific dates or erase them and forget them and start with a clean slate. Only you can make yourself feel guilty, and only you can resolve that source of defeat in your life. That's what forgiveness is all about.

Let us list for you a few recent opportunities for entertaining. For example, we felt the desire to help our elderly mothers see many of their old friends. A brunch or morning coffee was the perfect way to do this.

A single friend entertained by having others over for appetizers before going out for dinner or in for dessert after the game. Just one course is easier to manage, especially when there are limitations such as space, energy, or money.

A potluck salad luncheon attended by every woman of a church fellowship and her mother or daughter was an easy way to create cherished memories. This was a blessing for each of the generations.

One group of four couples dine together monthly, rotating homes and food assignments. They have discovered some wonderful new dishes and developed lasting friendships over the years.

What can you do to help prevent sibling rivalry when a new baby comes to the home? Jean's grandson, Erick, was the center of the celebration at "big brother's day" when newborn Grant was brought home from the hospital. Young Erick reported that the blue ribbon around the tree in the front yard was for him because he was now a big brother, and "I take care of Grant."

Many single male friends love to entertain, and some are really good cooks. Just being single, male, a senior citizen, inexperienced, or a person with limitations such as diabetes doesn't prevent entertaining if the motivation is there.

A negative self-image is the greatest hindrance to hospitality/entertaining. This insecurity causes us to need to impress others. Fear of rejection can paralyze us if we are obsessed with what we have, what we serve, or ourselves. Being overly concerned with a picture-perfect house or a meal for epicurean taste will lead to tension, anxiety, and fatigue, but worst of all, that "never-again" attitude.

We know that the Lord loves each person, and He wants us to love each other. We can't know and understand and be supportive of others unless we are healed by Him to accept who we ourselves are. Only then can we focus on the individuals He brings to our hearts to be loved in His name.

So where does this leave us—lonely singles, employed homemakers, frightened beginners, older adults, parents of preschool twins, and the seasoned hosts—all of whom could use 50-hour days, more essential skills, a bank full of money, and the energy of a junior high cheerleader? Is there a place for sharing ourselves and our homes on the list of our priorities? Perhaps as important: Is there a way to do it without either exhausting or bankrupting us? These are valid questions this book will attempt to answer.

3
Hospitality Is
a Family Affair

Couples where partners have identical social and personal needs are about as rare as albino peacocks! That means that a lot of communicating and negotiating needs to take place before congenial entertaining is possible and hospitality is genuine.

When you enter a home where tension is so thick you could slice it, no one has to broadcast it. How can anyone cheerfully welcome guests with an infectious smile and a happy heart unless there is harmony in the home?

In a family, life gets complicated, and that is an understatement! Each person has to blend his or her values and goals with everyone else's. As with a summit of nations, there may be stalemates or stormy debates before peace is achieved. Said emphatically and with clarity: Compromises must be made.

When there is enough trust that everyone knows each family member will get fair treatment, families can come up with some common goals. Ideally, every person's need to have friends into the home should be supported by other family members. Resources, including time, space, energy, and money, should be prorated in some sort of fair way.

Perhaps just sharing with your family your desires and urging them to express theirs will open the door to communicate easily. Then you can brainstorm what you'd like to do and come up with a plan to be supportive of each other.

No plan for the family is acceptable until every member says, "Yes, I can live with that." Also, no one can always be a taker, and no one can always be a giver without hurting the relationship. Everyone in the family deserves consideration.

Both of us have experienced conflicting needs with our husbands. We wives work with people and need more time for solitude than our husbands need. A part of one solution for more social interaction was for the husband to participate in his company's sports leagues. His joining a civic club also helped in balancing our desires to be with people.

Both husbands have felt that in order for us to get adequate rest and enjoy extra company too, they would do their share at home. This meant helping with routines and also with entertaining. Occasionally they have done the whole entertainment bit, just as many times we have done it alone. And that works. When the family members do share the entertaining effort, the burden is light.

I (Jean) remember a really wild year of intense work that was going to take every minute. Friend husband, Mr. Gregarious himself, had a less demanding schedule, and he was concerned that no friends would be invited to our home. So—are you ready for this?—this brave guy offered to do all the entertaining for a year! The condition was that it was completely his show. He wanted to do it "his way."

It was a bit scary because I cared about "my turf." But it was also delightful to behold. Husband listed all the people we wanted to invite and carefully grouped them in sixes. He developed a menu with a work plan that started two days ahead, planned a grocery order for his menu, and shopped. He planned to serve that menu every time company came . . . not a bad idea for a beginner!

Husband really did set a trial table for eight and was secure in sticking to it. He prepared all his recipes to check them out. Then he put his uncanny plan into action. (Skills in the working world are adaptive to home use too.)

I was to slave at my desk until guests were due, completely free of preparation concerns. At the appointed hour, I was to answer the door and recharge my batteries with a relaxing evening. Please note that I was to have no complaints.

No complaints included ignoring the dust on the chair rungs and some of the trivial things which only women seem to care about. But it worked—his way—and the whole thing was accomplished with such pride and excitement that incidentals like dust didn't matter.

You may be wondering if there were tensions—not really. At least not related to entertaining. We had planned our goals together. Sure, it took some concessions on the part of both of us. Husband gave his time to plan and do all the work; I had to be willing to let him do it his way with his standards and to fortify him with my supportive spirit. Being supportive is not as easy as it sounds. Letting go and letting someone else do it is even harder.

Now we both know that the other can perform in another role; I can function in the work world, and he can function equally well in the home. Didn't we say compromises were essential?

That year holds some treasured memories, partly because of the different persons we were able to enjoy in our home in spite of the stress of our personal schedules. Sometimes guests can be a needed therapy in a hectic routine.

There are many loving husbands who could not possibly

be that kind of help. They have other ways in which they excel, and that's fine. Love them for who they are! Some husbands couldn't handle it because of attitude, job demands, other priorities, lack of skill, or whatever. That's OK.

Neither they nor you should feel any pressure from our experience. The whole point is that if you're both open and sharing about your needs and feelings, there are acceptable ways of meeting everyone's needs. You should discover yours.

We have friends who have the most diverse needs of any "empty nest" couple we know. Scott is gone ten days every two weeks and comes home so exhausted that he prefers quiet times with a few close friends.

Emily, Scott's wife, a recluse during her intense hours of research, requires much social interaction and physical activity to satisfy her zest for living.

Through the years Emily has developed several good friends among women without husbands who share her interest in church, the community, and the arts. Often she arranges for them to have lunch together, to visit a museum, to go for a swim, or to work together on a common cause. Or she simply calls someone and invites her over for coffee on a bleak winter day.

But Emily's priority when Scott is home is to be with him. They love their lake retreat where friends are often invited to join them. They'd both choose an easier life-style, but with their "givens" they have worked out a solution they can live with and enjoy.

We all have to live with our "givens" or circumstances. Work requirements, physical limitations, a parent living with us, and other things affect our total lives, including how we can entertain our family and friends.

One "given" that varies in every home is our own personalities. If either partner is pushed beyond his or her tolerance to be with people, company can become a bondage. When either spouse doesn't choose to or can't be a part of having guests in the home, then the other must be very understanding and creative in order to be fulfilled in a way not destructive to the marriage.

Realize that it is not selfish to do things separately. In fact, when we part from time to time to do things that re-create us, we come back together with a freshness and joy.

Your "given" may be that you are not the traditional family of two parents and two children in the home (only 7 percent are!). But you who are single parents, older, handicapped, or whatever, have exactly the same needs for friendship and social interaction that anyone else has. Often resources—energy, money, space, etc.—are limited, and you wonder how you can entertain. If housing is shared, you also have to work together to create a plan that will be mutually satisfying. We will list suggestions for "how you can" in another chapter.

Kids Count, Too

Obviously, when children are in the home, they count too. There isn't a better place anywhere for them to learn the social skills that will help them be secure and at ease all their lives. Also, if parents have a hospitable nature, it is only natural for the kids to exhibit those same characteristics. Attitudes are "caught," not "taught."

Of course, what's fun for one may be a "drag" for another. We don't have to feel so much togetherness that we can't do things apart. If Mom and Dad want a relaxing dinner and good conversation with their friends, it's OK for the Brownie bunch to have a tray in the family room. Or perhaps the older teens would rather go out for a pizza—they know their own time is coming.

So, when the high school crowd is in for chili after the game, Mom and Dad may be the kitchen support, but they don't have to try to be the ping-pong champions. The golden rule should work at home foremost.

When you have your own family goals worked out, they may look like this:

Mom and Dad—guests once a month
             —be available to respond to special needs
Highschoolers—two parties a year (their choice)
Gradeschooler—one slumber party
            —a birthday party
            —may have an overnight guest when Mom and Dad have planned company
Whole family—holidays, family reunions, vacations, cookouts with neighbors, and special family celebrations.

This month's goal might be:

June 7—Invite new neighbors and the Osters, 12:30 lunch on the deck. Grill hamburgers, include kids (ten persons total). Try new basketball goal. Crank freezer of ice cream.

And Outside Your Home

Since the spirit of sharing yourself with others isn't confined to your home, you are equally hospitable whether you invite the lonely senior citizen to ride with you to the Farmer's Market, take her home to share your day, or carry your soup pot to her house to share your lunch.

There are times when you want to be hospitable and it simply makes more sense to carry the casserole to a grieving family or take someone to a restaurant. In fact, a working woman may find noon hours to be the perfect time to be hospitable. Don't hesitate to do it, but avoid the trap of always eating out simply because it's easier. After a while you'll lose your memories of shared joy in your home.

Actually, in its totality, being hospitable means being willing to go to someone else's home when you would rather stay at home. Since hospitality involves giving of self, it takes on many forms for all of us.

Our big family has been faced with Mother's physical inability to be hostess to us all at holiday times. We've carried food in, taken her to our homes in turn, and done everything but resort to restaurants. There is no easy way, especially now with the infant great-grandchildren.

But Mother's physical needs are no more important than her emotional needs. Sometimes, even when it exhausts her, she needs to see the tables full and feel the joy of being surrounded by family in her own home. We must occasionally allow her this. While it is inconvenient to all of us, it blesses us, too, and gives the children a lifetime memory to cherish.

When we get right down to it, nothing on earth matters but relationships: the vertical one to our Father and the horizontal ones to our family and friends (is this symbolic of the cross?). Loving each other is what it's all about, and love is something you do.

4
Lee: A Paradox

We want you to know Lee—she's real and very close to our hearts. To help us to be accurate in our description of her, let's spend a typical day with her. As reporters, hopefully we're unbiased; we admit it's not always easy to be objective.

"Sure, you can follow me around a day if you want, but you might think you're at the zoo," Lee joked in response to our request to observe her for a day.

Lee is an enigma, in her late twenties and lean of muscle; assertive but modest about herself; enthusiastic yet with a quiet inner being; loves quality but shops garage sales and settles for secondhand when necessary; nutrition conscious but willing to bend for special times; full-time homemaker but earns money with infrequent private duty nursing or selling unique handcrafts; turned off by "soaps" and most mind wasters but tolerant of those who are so inclined; fun loving and God fearing. But Lee's not perfect; what human is?

You say you would like to meet her? Perhaps you have, and she lives right next door. For us, this day of observing renewed our faith in the future.

"Hi, come in. How about coffee with me? Tony just left for work, and the kids are getting dressed," she said with a big smile. We wondered how smiling we would be to put up with visitors this early in the day. Lee helped the smallest one with his shoes and gave him a hug.

Filling our cups, Lee explained, "I only allow myself two cups—early in the day. I'm struggling to cut down because I was drowning in coffee. That's a holdover from working days."

"Lee, your house is so neat—we hope you didn't straighten up for us?" we asked as we sipped the fragrant hot liquid.

"Oh, no, I haven't done a thing but get dressed and prepare breakfast. We make it a practice to pick up things before going to bed at night. The kids have to pick up their own mess—even the bathroom. They're pretty good even for their age. We've always made a game of it." Lee explained, "You're going to see us as we really are."

"The first thing I have to take care of this morning are the bills and business. Tony works extra on Saturdays, and I do the paperwork and the tax stuff and take care of all the checks. It saves him time. Tony wants me to be able to handle all the family business should anything happen to him. Do you agree that's a good idea?" she asked.

"Of course we do. We heard you're equally at home with a 1040 form or a yummy homemade cheesecake. That's great," we replied.

The children required intermittent attention throughout the morning, but finally Lee said, "I'm ready to plan dinner. I do it before lunch, so if I can do two things at once, I do. I want to wash all the salad things, put in separate plastic bags and chill. Our couple's Bible study is having a potluck dinner tonight. I'm taking the salad, two dressings, and cheese bread. The cheese bread is frozen," Lee said.

Lee prepared soup, sandwiches, and fruit for herself and the two boys. We had insisted on bringing our brown bag lunches. With the salad ingredients ready in the fridge, Lee got out her recipes for the two dressings and quickly made French and a sweet-sour dressing using the food processor. She capped each in a pint jar, ready to carry to church.

Frequently Lee checked her daily "do" list. "Before I clean up this mess, I want to start a carrot cake to freeze for our guests this weekend." She continued, "I'll freeze the layers of cake but not ice it until I'm ready to use it." That was a smart idea. Cakes freeze well, but icings usually don't.

"I make double or triple recipes of many things which require lots of time, like soup or chili, and then have them for an easy meal later, like the soup today. Usually, when we have company, the main dish is frozen, ready to heat," Lee said, "and I'm not above mixes or the deli if I have to use them."

Lee finished cleaning the mess in the sink and said, "Now's my handwork time, so we can move to the den. I sell craft items at a local boutique. Usually I can work an hour a day on this, but sometimes I nap instead . . . especially if it's going to be a long evening."

"Lee, do you have any special secrets to share with our readers?" we queried.

"Well, not really. I do use every bit of help I can get. For example, I don't have lots of gadgets or fancy equipment but really use what I have. I like to sew, but I restrict myself to something very special for me or gifts and crafts I can sell. Otherwise I could get carried away with it," she said with a smile, adding, "I keep trying to learn better ways to do everything. There really is a lot of help for anyone who looks for it, you know."

"What kinds of help?" we asked.

Lee answered, "When I take the boys to the story hour at the public library, I read or check out books for myself.

Then there is the extension service and the newspaper, as well as adult education courses. Last fall I took a night course in upholstery and re-covered those two den chairs."

"Pardon me," Lee said, "while I listen to the phone tapes. I put it on the answering switch when you rang the doorbell this morning. I need to listen to know if there is anything that won't wait until tomorrow," she explained.

In the meantime, the buzzer went off on the automatic oven. Lee removed the cake pans from the oven and also removed two large loaves of cheese bread from the freezer to thaw for tonight. Unhappily for Lee, both cakes were lopsided and would need some special help from the icing. Oh, well! Lee scratched the carrot cake and bread from her "do list."

Lee had barely gotten the handwork out to show us (a blessing done in counted cross-stitch) when the two boys came in, wide awake. "OK, you know the rules—if you don't sleep, you still have to stay in bed until two anyway. Let's go back. I'll get you up for the library hour, I promise," Lee told them, singing as she led them back to their "castles."

Coming back to the den, Lee said, "The Lord has been so good to us. Those kids are such a joy. If they could just stay little forever . . ." she added, "We started them with regular naps and bedtimes at night. They play hard and need that long sleep. I'm afraid I need their naptimes too."

That remark led to another question: "Lee, do you miss your busy life as a surgical nurse?"

"Yes, I do," she replied. "It was very difficult at first, and I still miss being in the midst of all that activity and being with the other professionals. But I made my choice and generally have no regrets. Perhaps this is one reason I've developed several creative outlets. But if I'm not careful, I could go overboard!"

The day was over and we were tired, but Lee appeared fresh and at peace with her world. The children were bubbling with their new library books under their arms. "We read a lot," explained Lee. "I'm not hung up on TV, so I seldom turn it on. The kids would rather have us. Do you think they'll remember our quiet times together?" she wished more than asked. Lee admits that sometimes she has to punish the boys for disobedience. But she does try not to let her own anger determine how she punishes.

As we prepared to leave and let Lee get ready for their church potluck, she reminded us, "You've commented on how well we've managed, to have this house, the furnishings, and all with just one job. You know, we figured we'd earn more with Tony's extra day of work and my occasional night of special duty, plus the seasonal handwork sales, than if I worked full-time and added those expenses."

"We think this is best for us and we hope to be able to keep it up, at least while the children are young," Lee said. "But we really have to work at it and watch our expenses carefully."

"Give us some examples, Lee," we asked.

"Well, we rarely eat out, so we do a lot of entertaining here at home. Often we have one or two couples in for games and dessert after the kids are asleep."

"The backyard is perfect for large groups, and the kids have the large play equipment out there. Or a chili buffet supper by the fire in winter is fun. Usually all the kids are included but not always." Lee thoughtfully added, "Mostly, we have simple things which don't cost a lot and can be prepared ahead of time."

"Another thing is that we don't buy on credit, except the

house. If we can't pay for it, we wait," Lee said, pausing for us to take it all in.

Lastly Lee added, "The Lord has blessed us, and He is really our security."

When we mentioned to an older friend, Ginny, what a delightful day this young mother had shown us, Ginny said, "Oh, I know your Lee. She's positively a jewel! I've seen her take a bit of nothing and make a precious centerpiece for a shower table."

Ginny further volunteered, "Lee makes it seem so easy to do things right. Best of all, she seems so full of love."

Yes, we think we know today's counterpart of the classic woman in Proverbs 31, and there are many more of you out there just like her. Not a parable but certainly a twentieth century paradox. Jesus knows you too—each by name!

5
Decently and in Order

The piercing sound of the phone jolted the otherwise lazy summer evening. An ordinarily vivacious and self-controlled young friend lost no time in getting to the point: "I need help!"

"I'm going to choke John when this is over, but I don't have time for that till Saturday. That character has put his whole career on the line by asking his boss and a visiting management team over tomorrow night for a cookout. They want the visitors to meet some of the younger company executives in a more informal setting." Kathryn continued, "I'm ready to panic. Where on earth do I start to do all this in just one day?"

"Well, maybe you'd feel better if you started by realizing what a lot of faith John has in you. He knows you can do it, but it will take careful planning," I replied.

"I've just coauthored a short summary that's the foundation for helping to keep our homes 'decently and in order.' It's partly for entertaining and partly just for keeping our sanity," was my response. "Maybe you'd better read it."

However, Kathryn, who felt the sands of time were running out at rocket speed, had but one thing on her mind right then. "Is the reading very long?"

"No, it will just take a few minutes. Besides, you'll have

some questions, and you know five minutes of planning's worth an hour of work. I'm free. Can you come over now?"

A much calmer friend answered, "I'm on my way!"

Twenty minutes later she had quickly read the list of management basics for keeping the home "decently and in order." I marked with a red pencil those sections which were particularly meaningful right now. "Now, Kathryn, let's get down to some specifics. You need to think about guests, possible weather problems, your menu and shopping list, preparation time needed, and available resources or help."

"Let's start with guests. How many are you expecting?" Kathryn counted on her fingers and wrote down twenty.

"There are six local couples besides John and me and six persons from out of town," she said. "Those from out of town are from various parts of the country."

"OK, then let's think about the menu next. What do you feel comfortable preparing for a cookout when it's just family?" was my next question.

"Oh, I usually barbecue chicken and have baked beans or potato salad and maybe some kind of hot bread. We usually don't have dessert, but I suppose we should with guests. Is barbecued chicken sophisticated enough for this 'VIP' group?" Kathryn honestly questioned.

"Kathryn, the emphasis on such short notice should be your survival and the relaxed atmosphere of the group. Sure, the barbecued chicken would be just right for a cookout and would hold well if it has to. Most people like it, too."

"How about watermelon for dessert? It seems perfect for eating outside. Besides, if the group has been confined to indoors for several days in offices and meetings, they will enjoy a chance to unbend outdoors," I added.

"Gosh," Kathryn worried, "I'm not sure I can barbecue

that many chickens at one time. What other ideas do you have for me?"

"Let's see. Would you consider having Bob's Barbeque Pit do the chickens? His are always good. This would free you to do other things. You could even heat up your grill to keep them warm, and it would seem like you had slaved for hours."

"Oh, wouldn't that be cheating?" Kathryn quickly retorted, with her eyes expressing astonishment.

"Of course not," I answered. "Many people buy fried chicken from the fast food store and put it on their own platters; others get a deli tray of thinly sliced ham and meats and cheeses, transfer the food to their own trays, and add parsley and slices of lemon to give it a little pizzazz."

"One of my friends with a busy career attributes her success to living near an unusual carryout restaurant. We must use all our resources. Often survival is more important than having made it from scratch!"

"Well, that's a great idea. This is beginning to sound manageable!" a relieved Kathryn replied. "I could get some fresh corn on the cob, too . . . some of these people probably never get good corn like I find at the Farmer's Market. If I get there early in the morning, it's always fresh."

"Right! Now start your shopping list, in the order of what needs to be done first. And probably the first thing will be to call Bob's and place an order for those chickens. Undoubtedly tomorrow, John could stop at Bob's and pick up the chickens on his way home from the office."

Kathryn wrote down the menu and the shopping order beside it, with the time to do each thing, so she could check it several times tomorrow.

Things were fast falling into place. "Do you need to bor-

row anything or ask anyone to help with anything, Kathryn?" I questioned.

"Yes, I do. I have to ask the personnel manager's wife to
bring folding chairs. I'll call her right now if I may?"

"Sure, help yourself," I said to the empty air, for she was
already dialing the kitchen phone. Kathryn had entertained
some before but never such an impressive group on such
short notice. But she was learning that entertaining can be
as informal as a spur-of-the-moment summer cookout as
well as the traditional holiday dinner. For either, extra help
or other resources should be used if they are available. Regardless, specific planning is always necessary.

"Guess what," Kathryn beamed as she hung up the
phone. "Myra volunteered to bring the dessert. I suggested
melons, and she will bring three nice big ones, already
chilled. That will help loads."

"What will happen if there is rain or the weather simply
turns into a disaster?" I asked, realizing that's always a possi-
bility, and you need an alternative plan for eating outside.
(I've learned this one the hard way!)

"That's no problem," Kathryn replied, "we have that
large screened area with a Ping-Pong table. I could cover
it with my huge checked gingham cloth. That and two card
tables with matching cloths would do nicely."

With six extra local spouses, I suggested that Kathryn
write out some duties on three-by-five-inch cards and let
them choose a "let-me-help" card. Such things as pouring
and refilling beverages and ice or serving the homemade
bread or cutting the melons could be included. This little
"card trick" gets help done with a minimum of confusion!
I've used it many times, and it always works. The men
usually take a card too.

If Kathryn were having a more formal dinner indoors, she

would need to think through her type of service. Buffet
service is easy in many homes. Family style is acceptable for
smaller groups, or having the host serve the plates from one
end of the table is preferred by many. The menu usually
determines the type of service, space, and equipment
needed.

As Kathryn finished looking at her menu and plans, I
suggested, "Run through your entire menu in your mind
now as if you were eating; it will remind you of things you
may have forgotten."

"Sure. Oh, yes, appetizers," said Kathryn, "what about
appetizers? Do I need them?"

"Only if you think you need them or there may be waiting time," was my response.

"No, I think not this time. The main group will have eaten
a nice seafood salad luncheon anyway. I'll just have something for them to drink," Kathryn replied, "but I see the
point of mentally going through the menu. It does help you
see the trouble spots. What else do I need to think about?"

"Why not mull over the preparation activities? You might
sleep better tonight. Here are some things to think about:

*dishes out and arranged according to serving plan
*tables prepared as much as possible
*all cleanup possible taken care of ahead of time
*a plan for after meal cleanup

It will be easier with the eating outside; however, you
need to think about clean plastic liners for the trash cans
(for corn cobs, melon rinds, and paper products). You may
wish to dampen hand towels or napkins or paper towels for
personal cleanup after barbecue and corn."

"Also, what about the house, especially the bathrooms?
Do these need any attention tomorrow? Who can clean
them and when?" were my latest questions.

"Wow, I hadn't even thought of all these things," Kathryn said and made a face, "but I surely would have thought of them tomorrow. I'll follow your suggestions and enlist the family for the house and outside chores. John is more than eager to do his share with this sudden 'crisis,' and even young Gwen can do a lot. John is doing the outdoor areas now."

"Now you're learning, Kathryn, that hospitality really is a family affair. By the way, save your receipts from your purchases. You should be able to use these expenses as business deductions."

"Well, we've been planning for an hour. Do you feel you can manage now?"

"I sure do, all thanks to you. Let's run through this menu again to make sure I have it all together, OK?" Kathryn said as she got her papers together.

The phone rang then, and one of Kathryn's friends asked for her. Amy called to tell her she would bring homemade bread for the cookout. So Kathryn happily scratched that item from her list. To recap, the following was Kathryn's revised plan for dinner at 7:00 PM:

Barbecued chicken—ten chickens to be picked up by John at six—(call Bob's tonight to place order; ask for extra sauce). (John will be in charge of the grill and serving chicken.)

Baked beans—four large cans of pork and beans. ("Doctor up" with sauteed onions, brown sugar, mustard, and barbecue sauce—one to one and one-half hours in largest casserole at 5:00 PM.)

Corn on the Cob—Buy two dozen ears of corn at Farmer's Market. Shuck corn by 3:00 PM, wrap in plastic, chill; borrow canner to boil corn. (Corn goes in boiling water after guests arrive.)

Pickles, tomatoes, green onions, and relishes (prepared by 4:00 PM and in fridge). Buy tomatoes, onions, and pickles at market.

Hot homemade bread (brought by Amy and Donald).

Chilled watermelon slices (brought by Myra and Tom).

Iced tea/coffee (make tea by noon; plug in large urn of coffee at 6:30). (Nancy and Ted volunteered to bring bags of ice and a cooler with soft drinks and fresh juices.)

Probably Kathryn wouldn't always write out a detailed menu plan, but with the limited time and number of persons involved, it was the only safe thing to do. The two of us use lists constantly, and often we find this prevents a pleasant dream from turning into a nightmare!

"I feel set free now," Kathryn said as she left. "I won't choke John after all! He may only owe me a night out."

"Right, and most of all, we want you and John to treasure this time and remember it with special happiness."

"And don't try to impress anyone. Remember when we open our home to others, especially strangers, we invite them to share a part of our private lives. You've paid them a compliment to invite them, and they are returning it to be there. Now, go and enjoy," were my parting words.

Two days later Kathryn reported the outcome of the cookout. "Everyone helped. I didn't have to do much after the guests arrived except be hospitable. It was amazing!"

Kathryn shared, "I wouldn't change a thing—it wasn't a stuffy 'one more meeting' but just a relaxing time of getting to know each other. I'll have to admit I'm wiped out today, but I'll be fine by tomorrow. Thanks again for all that coaching."

Since that successful event, John has been recommended
for a promotion, although nothing was said about his family
and their entertaining talents!

Both John and Kathryn have decided that if they can be
hospitable for business purposes, they should do it for other
reasons too. They invited their Sunday School class for
homemade ice cream, and next on the calendar is a chili
supper for Gwen's Brownie troop. The whole family is enjoying this together.

Now let's return to that list of "Decently and in Order"
which I gave to Kathryn when planning her big event.

The list may seem long and tedious, but it isn't. Most of
these ideas are not original or new. They're simply a result
of the school of experience. Maybe you can skip some
grades!

"Decently and in Order"

There really is a biblical admonition to have a well-
managed home. The older women are told to teach the
younger ones: nothing profound, exotic, or complex but
that which will help them to be more committed to family
and home. Volumes could be written, but:

I. Planning Is Essential

A. Plan what you wish to accomplish. Write it down.

How long will it take? What can be eliminated? What is
my real goal . . . a spotless house or more time to enjoy all
our family and friends? People are more important than
ideal arrangements.

B. Plan for the expected.

Anticipate demands on your time—check them out and determine what is possible for you. Accept interruptions as normal. Avoid waiting until the last minute for any anticipated task. Keep extras of routinely used items and first-aid supplies on hand.

C. Plan for the unexpected.

Anticipate drop-in guests, especially at holiday and special times. Build in a time cushion to enjoy the unexpected. Consider waiting time a gift and relax, read, do handwork, write notes, do exercises, or pray.

II. Establish Priorities

A. Accept reality.

You have human and financial limitations. Prioritizing is simply making choices. You may need to lower your standards. Remember that sometimes, survival is victory!

B. Communicate with your family or household.

Be open. Reveal your honest feelings and desires. Encourage others to be open. Reach compromises to enable everyone to have their most important desires met in an appropriate way. Commit yourselves to helping each other entertain, so the hosts can enjoy the guests.

C. Establish ground rules for all family members to follow.

Decide how to share housekeeping responsibilities, rotating chores to learn all skills and eliminate boredom. Decide that family members routinely care for their rooms and pick up after themselves. The motto: "Put it up before you put it down" is a good one. Establish rules for controlling time wasters, such as excessive TV, telephone, etc. Everyone over four or five years old cleans the bathroom after using it.

D. Prioritize.

Decide exactly what your priorities are, as individuals and as a family. Combine the various lists into a master family list so they are not in conflict. Start with number one on your list every day. When finished, do number two, etc. Say no to things you should not or cannot do. Allow time for yourself. No one else can keep you in vibrant physical, spiritual, mental, social good health.

III. Organize for Efficiency

A. Develop routines.

Routines require no decision making and cause no stress. Everyone can be depended on to do their share. Clean on schedule, not before company. Organize lists for daily, weekly, and seasonal jobs. Straighten house every night before going to bed. Do some cleaning daily. Then unexpected guests won't be a crisis.

B. Improve work techniques.

Alternate liked and unliked jobs. Be open to learning better ways. See what can be eliminated, simplified, or speeded up. Learn what different soils collect in your home and what cleaning products get rid of them best. Put out doormats and otherwise manage to keep dirt out. Use exhaust fan over the range when cooking. Do one job until finished instead of hopping from one to another. Use lists, trays, and cleaning-supply caddies. Keep tools and equipment in good working condition. Keep equipment stored where easily accessible and use it.

C. Plan a place for everything and keep it there.

Establish an out-of-sight, long-term storage area. Put shelves and hooks where needed. Store items near place of use. Have containers where clutter collects—toybox, newspaper basket, mail, etc. Get rid of things no one cares enough about to be responsible for (this might include pets!).

D. Combine or group jobs together.

Plan menu and grocery order while cleaning fridge. Clean bedroom while bedding is being laundered. Keep mending by the TV. Never put away a garment unless it is ready to wear. Have telephone near other work (mending, cooking, etc.) Double or triple recipes for casseroles, soups, chili, and freeze excess. Always check food storage areas before shopping.

E. Eliminate jobs.

Let dishes air dry (more economical with a dishwasher too). Put collections that have to be dusted together under glass. Use one or two big plants rather than many smaller ones. Hang dried clothing at once to eliminate wrinkles. Buy permanent press that requires no ironing and hang or fold immediately when finished drying. Reevaluate your standards. What can you do less often or not at all? Refuse to do unnecessary tasks.

F. Use shortcuts.

Make week's sandwiches and cupcakes one day, label and freeze. Cook and bake in quantity, freeze some. Freeze measured quantities of chopped onions, peppers, bread crumbs, grated cheese, etc. for quick use. Learn to eliminate use of pans by putting crackers or nuts in a plastic sack

and roll for crumbs, or let dough rise in a large plastic bag.
Use freezer to oven tableware to eliminate dishes and dish-
washing. Line casseroles with foil before filling for freezing. When frozen, remove, wrap, and label. Later bake and
serve in that dish.

G. Evaluate the true cost of some services.

A resource (time, money, energy) used for one thing is
then not available for something else. Hiring a baby-sitter
or exchanging sitting may help prevent the divorce court.
Hiring a teenager for lawn care or snow removal may be
wiser than chancing a cardiac arrest. A deli specialty is
cheaper than taking off work half a day to cook for an
impromptu potluck. Bartering or trading services may be
possible and helpful to two different families. Sometimes
paper products may be the only logical choice.

H. Keep it simple.

Impressing people isn't important. Making people feel
welcome and loved is. Try entertaining with potluck, dessert parties, casseroles and salad, breakfast, snacks after the
game, or an evening at church. Use recipes which you make
easily. Plan menus possible to serve with the dishes and
facilities you have. Mugs of soup or chili, dessert or hot
popcorn, or simply a freezer of ice cream can be a fellowship feast. Deli trays or fast food items, when garnished with
a special touch, can turn impossible into possible.

I. Keep a good file.

File copies of favorite, easy do-ahead recipes and menus.
Copy any good idea from any source. (Good ideas don't
belong to anyone!) Keep a record of friend's preferences,
allergies, birthdates, etc. Develop a repertoire of several
menus which are especially easy for you and your family.

Write on cards, with a shopping list, names of persons invited for that specialty and date. Recycling an idea for another time makes sense.

IV. Beyond the Basics

A. Further notes.

Do as much ahead as possible. Look for freezer recipes to make before the big day. If you have a natural flair and want to do something special such as a fun centerpiece, do it (but do it ahead of time). It is not necessary, however. If you wish, an unusual ceramic or accessory gives that exotic touch and a simple garnish on a plate enhances both the flavor and the appearance.

B. Assistance.

Use all the help that is available. Utilize your family and guests. Place on the counter three-by-five cards with jobs listed, stacked in order to be done. When someone says, "May I help?" ask the volunteer to do what is listed on the top card.

C. Just you.

Plan your work for your most productive time of the day, depending on whether you are a "lark" or an "owl," and wear comfortable shoes while working. If possible, before guests arrive take time to bathe and relax a bit.

D. The heart of the matter.

Take a minute before guests arrive to hug your family and tell them how much you appreciate them. No guest is more important than the family you love. At some point in this special time, breathe a prayer of thanksgiving and ask

God's blessing on every relationship coming together in
your home.

    E. As the guests drive up.

Fill the kitchen sink with hot soapy water at the last
minute to soak pots and pans and help in the later cleanup.
Now relax. Absolutely nothing can come up that basic good
manners can't handle. If something isn't perfect, call on
your sense of humor. Enjoy yourselves—that's the purpose
of the whole thing! When the guests are gone, assess the
evening and thank your family for the time shared with
others.

6
The Kitchen Area

Some kitchens are planned and furnished so well that working in them seems almost effortless, but you may become irritated in another kitchen even if all you want to do is to make a cup of tea. Your first step to enjoying cooking is to organize your kitchen and serving areas so you can work without frustration.

The two essential activities to plan for in a kitchen are food preparation and cleanup. But you may also want to use your kitchen for eating, planning, chatting, laundering, keeping records, food preservation, or children's play. Whatever the use, good light, ventilation, convenient safe wiring, adequate work space, easily cleaned surfaces, and organized storage all contribute to your pleasure and should be your goals.

It seems almost elementary to say it, but ideally every kitchen needs at least three work centers for efficiency:

The Sink-Dishwasher Center
Around the sink and dishwasher should be two to three feet of counter space on each side. Stored under or above should be items used first at the sink such as detergents, pans, knives, and dish towels. Dishes should be stored between the sink and eating areas.

The Range Center

The range center surrounds the range or surface burners but not a built-in oven. Counter space on either side of the range adds more convenience. Store other pans, frying pans, and cooking tools. Some foods which are not damaged by heat and may be stored at the range center are cereals and crackers. If the oven is built in there should be at least a small counter beside it.

Mixing and Food Storage Center

A mixing and food storage center is where food is prepared for cooking, baking, chilling, freezing, or eating. Three feet of counter space is minimum, and more is desirable if much cooking or baking is done. Provide storage here for baking dishes, canisters, packaged and canned foods, mixing tools, and small appliances.

Much more detail could be written about the work centers, but this will get you started on kitchen arrangement. The smaller the kitchen, the more essential it is to have the areas defined and organized. If you need to do more than minor rearranging, there are many helpful resources in your county extension office, public library, magazines, or books. Take advantage of this information. Of course, a commercial kitchen planning firm could handle the task, but for a fee. Considering the hours you spend in the kitchen, it should be a satisfying place in which to work.

The Essentials

It isn't necessary to own every small appliance, tool, serving piece, or special item. You may never use a fondue pot or tiered cake pans. Many items you own are probably used only a few times a year, if that often. Take inventory, and give up those things you really don't need. Store the seldom-used and seasonal things on the very high shelves or in the out-of-the-way storage areas of the basement, garage, or wherever.

Now examine what you have left in your possession. Is each item in good working condition? If not, can it be repaired or sharpened? Should it be replaced? The efficient kitchen has:

    sharp knives
    a workable can opener
    one or more rubber scrapers
    several measuring cups for liquids and solids
    measuring spoons
    vegetable peeler
    cutting board(s)
    mixing bowls
    pots and pans (with lids which fit and flat bottoms which fit the size of the burners)
    baking dishes and casseroles
    cooking tools
    refrigerator/freezer storage dishes
    sifter
    wooden spoons
    containers or canisters for staples
    foil and plastic wraps
    cleaning supplies
    and whatever else you need

We cook so differently and have such individual tastes and life-styles that one person's luxury is absolutely essential to another. There is no right or wrong. Carefully consider what you buy or ask others to give you. Study the cost, care, storage, and whether you'll use it often enough to make owning it worthwhile. It might be wise for the bride to wait until she has kept house for some time before deciding on

expensive items such as china, silver, crystal, or some appliances. Admittedly, this is radical thinking, but our tastes
and living situations often change dramatically in just a few
short years.

Create a Table Setting

If you wait until you own twelve place settings of bone
china and sterling flatware to entertain, you never will.
While the whole point of true hospitality is loving people
and making them welcome, we still like to do the best we
can to honor our guests by setting an attractive table. This
doesn't have to be extravagant. It's just "icing on the cake."

Before you have everything you will ever want to own,
it is helpful to have complete sets of something to use. It is
OK if your stemware is glass, your flatware is stainless, and
the dishes are the least expensive you can find. Your table
still can be set with flair.

• *Use color.* Choose dishes, glasses, candles, and linens
in a color scheme you love. Try to buy everything in that
color scheme so you can mix and match. After all, beautiful
colors don't cost any more than insipid ones.

• *Use contrast.* White dishes on a white cloth can be
drab, drab. But the same dishes on a navy cloth are pure
drama. Emerald green or plaid napkins in navy and white
would add another spark.

• *Add pattern.* Pattern piques interest but can be over-
done and can become boring over time. Dishes with a bold
pattern are best on a solid-colored cloth. Arrange patterned
dishes so that the design is consistent or right side up. If the
dishes are plain, use the patterns, colors, and textures of the
centerpiece or linens to create interest.

• *Use things in unusual ways.* Bandanas serve well as
napkins for a cookout; bricks can be used as a base for a

multileveled centerpiece for a casual buffet; any small col-
lection sparks conversation when used as a table decoration;
fiber fans, mirror tiles, or guest towels make interesting
placemats; and fishing lures, seashells, and a bit of fishnet
coordinate the mood when food comes from the waters.
Harmonize your creativity with your possessions.

● *Centerpieces.* A grouping of votive candles in any odd
stemware on a mirror costs little and gives the added delight of reflected candlelight. Three fresh flowers added to
a small planter of greenery infuses new life. A bowl of fruit,
fresh garden flowers, a figurine, or a cornucopia of autumn's
abundance of vegetables, gourds, nuts, and leaves are perfect for the table. Do you long to capture the essence of
Christmas in your December decorating? The fragrance of
evergreens and pinecones plus the glow of colorful candles
are incomparable for this.

● *Use your imagination.* For example, skip the plates
and serve a sandwich on a napkin-lined, woven paper plate
holder. Tie napkins with ribbon bows, or simply tie a napkin
in a loose knot and arrange it above the plate. Sack lunches
tied with bright yarn thrill the kids at a park party.

It's easier to encourage mixing among people who don't
know each other well if you serve food throughout the
house, using hall tables, dressers, coffee tables, and card
tables as buffets. Finger foods, beverages, plates, and napkins are easily located here, but it's a good idea to save the
messy stuff for the kitchen or dining room.

● *Extend what you have.* You can use dishes from different sets on the table if they coordinate well. When you
have more guests than dishes, renting often is as reasonable
as buying quality paper products. Borrowing is all right if
you have that kind of relationship with someone. Or use the
disposable products. When you make the best decision pos-

sible, then dismiss it from your mind while you concentrate
on the more important things.

  • *Don't fear the "rules."* Plan for everyone's comfort
and happiness . . . yours and your guests. That will take care
of any rules you need to know.

7
Kitchen Capers

If you've ever lived in a rural area where markets are miles away or in a far country where markets are extremely limited, you quickly developed an appreciation for having the food and supplies you needed to have on hand. It made you plan carefully and well ahead. It also sharpened your skills in making do—or doing without.

Jean remembers requesting a dessert recipe from her American hostess when she first arrived in Nairobi, Kenya. When the recipe was mailed to her later, there were six substitutions noted. After 1 cup pecans, the hostess wrote, "I use cashews," after cornstarch, "Here we use corn flour," and for brown sugar, "We use date palm sugar," etc. After some practice, most recipes can be approximated with locally available ingredients.

Your kitchen has in it the basic for many wonderful feasts. Written recipes are simply someone's experiment—planned or otherwise—that turned out well. Using tables of equivalents will help you use cocoa and margarine instead of running out to buy cooking chocolate. Using logic will allow you to substitute your abundance of garden tomatoes for canned paste when you make spaghetti sauce. Using your imagination will allow you to combine a sauce with a protein and vegetables to prepare a tasty new casserole.

You are the creator in your kitchen. Feel free to adapt good ideas. For example, the beautiful thumbprint Christmas cookies are simply little balls of sugar cookie dough flattened with a dent in the middle for filling with red and green jelly: easy, pretty, and sweet. Perhaps, though, you want a Christmas appetizer that's different this year. You like the look of the thumbprint cookie, but you don't want the sweetness. Why not use the recipe for cheese straws and fill the thumbprints with red-and-green hot pepper jelly? A great flavor combination, and it is your own creation.

An attitude of experimenting with foods is a bit like the attitudes of tourists. Some Americans travel the world demanding hamburgers and steak. But others seek out the unique dishes of the countries they visit. Some return home totally unaware of the delights they have missed, while the others have eaten some things they didn't care for. But they have discovered many wonderful foods and flavors they will enjoy forever.

In experimenting with foods and cooking techniques, you are risking a flop. But it is only one dish one time. Not only will you discover dishes you enjoy; you'll become self-assured and fulfilled. Your family, too, will enjoy the excitement of your creativity and will serve as your panel of judges.

There is a sense of joy when you feel in total control of your kitchen and home. Getting ready for guests is actually just a small part of running an efficient food system in your home. Every single day your family's nutritional needs must be met, their appetites satisfied, the budget balanced, and your love felt. For your own happiness you need to feel that you have some free time to do other things, so you must be able to manage and work efficiently and well in your kitchen. You need to know all the "tricks of the trade"!

You also want to be a winner in the stress of unexpected situations as well as in the special times you have planned and worked hard to be able to enjoy. You will be a winner if you have:

- developed efficient work skills
- arranged your kitchen logically
- mastered the use of your equipment
- become as organized as possible
- stored an emergency food supply, and
- used your creativity.

With all of these prepreparations, you have only to overcome self-doubt and fear. And you have no reason to fear, "For the Holy Spirit, God's gift, does not want you to be afraid of people, but to be wise and strong and to love them and enjoy being with them" (2 Tim. 1:7, TLB).

Developing efficient work skills is mainly a matter of awareness and desire. Be constantly on the lookout for how to do things better or faster. Omit or skip steps that are not absolutely necessary. Have a place for everything, and everything in its place. Clean up as you work. Understand and be able to do all cooking processes and techniques. Learn the principles of cooking with eggs, yeast, sauces, meat, etc. Watch other people work, and when they can do it better, change your ways. Enjoy excellence.

Mastering your equipment is a must. In fact, probably the first thing we should do is to get rid of anything we seldom use. The "gift of the year" is often an example of this. Tell your family that you have limited space and do not want any more kitchen gadgets unless you specifically request a particular one. Decide that you aren't going to waste your money on buying anything you don't plan to fully utilize. If you own it, make it work for you.

Have you mastered the automatic timer on your oven, wok, food processor, electric skillet, blender, or microwave oven? All are efficient. If you have any small appliance you haven't mastered, why not work with it for a few days until you can use it easily?

Use your equipment for multiple uses at one time to save washing. Plan to process from dry to wet. For example, to prepare foods for the freezer, do bread crumbs in the blender or food processor; then grate cheeses and follow that by chopping vegetables. Lastly, make a recipe of salad dressing or sauce. Most people dislike washing the equipment after just one small job, but this way you scrape the equipment with a rubber scraper between jobs and only wash your equipment once—not four times.

Obviously, those who own freezers, microwave ovens, and other miraculous kitchen helpers have a head start with any food preparation. Whether it's our family supper or a guest meal, we are hours ahead of where our grandmothers were with the equipment they owned.

Microwave Oven

One key to speed is for you to be able to use your microwave oven to full advantage. For microwave miracles, really understand how microwave works and when it is the ideal cooking method to use. Ideal uses include reheating everything, melting, cooking bacon, superb vegetables, crumb crusts and single-crust pies, chicken, fish, and baking potatoes. Casseroles can be adapted for microwave and made quickly by cooking each ingredient, combining and heating. If you only use your microwave to reheat leftovers, enroll in a good workshop and learn its potential. If that isn't possible, there are some great books available in your local library. It is easily mastered and well worth the effort to learn.

Slow Cookers

Almost the opposite of the microwave in its method, the slow cooker cooks for hours without needing any attention. It cooks one-dish meals, reheats rolls without drying them, bakes potatoes and breads, steams puddings, cooks tougher cuts of meat, cooks cereal overnight, makes fruit butters, and heats beverages, etc.

Special attention given to adding ingredients according to cooking time needed will make a perfect product. Adding beautifully colored vegetables for only the last hour of cooking time will prevent overcooking and loss of color. The same is true of fish and seafood. Milk should be added just before the end of cooking time.

Two and one-half hours of slow cooking equal one hour of cooking on high. If you wish to reduce liquid, take off the cover and turn up the heat.

Surprisingly enough, fuel costs for microwave and slow cookers are nearly identical, as total electricity used is very similar. One uses the oven so fast and the other so long.

Pressure Pan

The pressure pan, like the microwave oven, cuts cooking time significantly. One big difference is how a pressure pan will tenderize less tender cuts of meat. A good pressure pan can easily pay for itself in a year, and there is no danger if directions are followed exactly.

Freezer

Many people think of their freezers as a royal tomb—to be loaded with treasures and never to be robbed. Used this way, a freezer is an expensive 'white elephant.'

A freezer is economical because it:
- saves seasonal surpluses
- takes advantage of bargains or bulk purchases
- eliminates extra trips to the store
- allows leftovers to be used as planned overs
- saves time by allowing partial preparation (chopped, grated, measured, or cleaned ingredients)
- saves time by allowing total preparation (eat it frozen or thawed, or it needs only to be cooked or heated)
- keeps products such as grains and cereals from contamination (four days in freezer will kill any insect eggs which may be in the product)
- prevents powdered milk, seeds, nuts, coconut, etc. from becoming rancid or tasting old
- makes it possible for you to avoid stress. Freezing allows food to be prepared when convenient rather than as needed. Doubling or tripling recipes and partial or total preparation of many foods saves time and energy. It also allows emergency meals to be available.

Your freezer is fantastic, but remember that nothing comes out of it better than you put it in there.

To feast from the freezer:
1.   Food should be at its peak quality and wrapped to prevent dehydration (freezer burn).

2.   Food should be labeled so it won't get lost and dated
      to be used in sequence so nothing gets too old.

The following foods freeze well:
*   cookies, uniced cakes, sweet rolls, rolls, cupcakes,
    bread, fruit breads, fruit pies
*   sandwiches, spread with soft margarine or butter
    rather than mayonnaise or salad dressing
*   most casseroles can be frozen for a few weeks
*   meats, poultry, seafoods
*   fruits and vegetables
*   cooked sauces (spaghetti, chili, sloppy Joes)
*   buttered crumbs for casserole toppings; other stale
    bread for stuffing or pudding
*   minced celery leaves and parsley
*   butter and milk
*   sliced fruitcake, layered between waxed paper to be
    served immediately
*   extra ice, fancy ice ring
*   punch base, ready for the gingerale
*   strips of meat for stroganoff, stir fry
*   freezer desserts and salads

We offer the following freezing suggestions:
1.   Basically use a vapor-proof, airtight package.
2.   Package food according to how it will be reheated:
      freezer wrap for microwave, foil for oven, etc.
3.   When freezing a casserole, line the dish with heavy
      foil or plastic wrap and freeze. After it is frozen, lift
      the food and foil out of the dish, overwrap in freezer
      paper, seal, label, and return to freezer. The cas-
      seroles will retain the shape of the dish, and your
      dish is available for daily use.

4. Check a food preservation leaflet prior to preparing fruits and vegetables for freezing. Most fruits need sugar or a syrup cover, and most vegetables must be blanched.
5. Separately wrap and freeze extra waffles and French toast. Pop in the toaster when desired.
6. Herbs and spices may get stronger or change flavors in the freezer. Season cooked foods lightly and adjust when heated.
7. Slightly undercook for the freezer. Reheating will finish the cooking.
8. Fill TV dinner trays with your own leftovers for a fast meal.
9. Make sandwiches assembly-line fashion, spreading margarine instead of salad dressing on bread, so it won't get soggy. Wrap separately, label, and freeze. Lunch carriers can "choose one and run." The sandwiches will thaw by lunch. Do not freeze lettuce and tomatoes.
10. Also for lunch carriers, freeze cupcakes or cookies in individual freezer bags. They are neater to eat without icing.
11. Many salads and desserts can be made ahead and frozen. Try to keep one of each for an emergency.
12. Keep a freezer bag of ends and dried bits of cheese to grate for casseroles. Cheese will not slice after freezing. Grate or preslice.
13. Pie crusts can be left flat with double waxed paper and frozen in pizza boxes. Overwrap. Or shape the pastry in pie pans and freeze, well wrapped.

Other ideas for the freezer include:
Plan to buy a larger piece of meat or chicken and cut off

some bits, either before cooking or when rare. Freeze the pieces for later use in a stir-fry entrée. Later add fresh broccoli, cauliflower, onions, water chestnuts, and soy sauce, and serve with rice. The cut-up meat thaws quickly and is ideal for stir-fry recipes.

Buy specialty breads, or bake your own in small pans. When frozen, they are versatile to use sliced thin for quick sandwiches or to accompany a entrée or perhaps dessert. They also are wonderfully economical as thoughtful gifts.

Shape burgers and wrap between layers of waxed paper or foil so they can be easily separated. The burgers can be charcoaled rare and frozen; then simply heat thoroughly for an outdoor flavor. With buns frozen, these can be a quick answer for an unexpected meal . . . stretched with pork and beans from the pantry.

Keep a container of soup "fixings" in the freezer. Pour off excess vegetable or meat stocks, and add leftovers and everything you have which fits your tastes. Use each time you make soup or stew.

Avoid freezing the following: potatoes because they become mushy and grainy; hard-cooked egg whites because they toughen; mayonnaise (it separates, but salad dressing does not); excess foods which are always available at about the same price; and a lot of empty space. The cost is to keep the freezer at 0 degrees—whether full or empty.

A freezer should:
    not be close to a heat source.
    be cleaned when the frost accumulates to one-quarter inch.
    have a running inventory attached to the door.
    be reasonably full.
    contain dated, labeled, well-wrapped foods.

be arranged so oldest food is used first.

This is not nearly all that could be said about the few appliances we have mentioned, and there are dozens more. The principles are the same, however. There are complete encyclopedias on just the microwave oven, for instance. Your library can help you learn what you need to know.

We would like to comment on oven meals, however. Baking is the most expensive way to cook—unless you cook several things at once. Then it is your cheapest method as well as a time saver, convenient, and easily cleaned up if the baking dish is also a serving dish. To cook an oven meal, remember:

1. The meat, casserole, or main dish will determine the temperature you use.
2. Choose other foods that cook at or about the same temperature.
3. If the temperature needed varies only a little, set the thermostat in the middle and adjust cooking time.
4. Choose vegetables that bake well. When cut in pieces, they will cook faster.
5. Check oven and dishes to make sure all will fit.
6. Start with the food that cooks longest. Using a minute timer, add other foods so all come out together.
7. Foods can be prepared and refrigerated until time to bake (add extra time for refrigerated/frozen food).

Food Emergencies

Now let's plan for your next food emergency. If that shocks you, think about it. Most emergency situations can be anticipated; and if you plan for all possibilities, you will be able to meet whatever comes with poise.

List the food emergencies you have had. They probably include unexpected guests, needing a fast contribution for a potluck, getting home late to prepare a meal, being asked to serve several members of a youth choir at the end of the month when your purse is flat, or having your child's room mother call the week before the holidays for party refreshments.

What can you do about those?

For starters, let's take that last problem first, for it really can be anticipated. Any homeroom or scout troup or ball team runs on the food which moms fix. Actually, that's a very small price to pay for all the benefit your child receives, and you do want to make your treat very special. After all, your child's feelings are involved here.

Probably the best thing you can do for yourself and for your child is to "jump the gun" on the leaders and offer to provide a treat when it will be convenient for you. Early in the school year, call the room mother and offer to provide the Valentine treat for the class. She'll be delighted that you are so thoughtful, and when Christmastime comes, you are off the hook.

Your other option is to call the room mother in November and tell her that you're doing your holiday baking. Ask whether you can make some Christmas cookies to put in your freezer for the class party. Your child will adore you, and you will have survived the system.

Several loaves of nut bread in the freezer would serve

very well as a potluck food, hostess gift, or as you visit the bereaved. So would unbaked fruit pies, rolls of bake-and-serve cookies, homemade casseroles, frozen desserts, or sauces. These foods can easily be made in double portions with one destined for the freezer. Anything in the freezer that is ready to thaw/bake/eat helps in any crisis.

For other food emergencies, it is a good idea to have at least four easily and quickly prepared meals on hand. They can be freezer meals or shelf meals or a combination of both as long as they have a long storage life. When you know you can serve a complete meal in less than an hour, you can be relaxed and happy when your college buddy en route to Miami remembers that this is your town. You are free to impulsively say and really mean it, "Come on over for supper. We can't wait to see you."

Besides being lifesavers when unexpected guests come by, emergency meals remove the stress when your appointment runs late or there's any kind of crunch that makes it difficult to cope with the meal situation. But try not to fall back on these meals too often, or they won't be a welcome treat when you do prepare them in a flash.

An emergency shelf need not be a separate place in the pantry. Just know what your emergency menus are, and anytime you use one of the foods, replace it at the first opportunity. You will want to keep a good supply of staples, salad ingredients, cheese, milk, bread, fruit, and eggs. Ice cream in the freezer is always a good security blanket. Unannounced guests feel more imposing if you have to go to market to make purchases just for them.

What we would choose for an emergency menu might not appeal at all to you. That's fine. You can choose your own. However, these we are listing will get you gracefully through any emergency with guests or family.

We like:
1.   Chicken chow mein or chicken and dumplings
2.   Salmon loaf
3.   Spaghetti
4.   Ham and sweet potatoes
5.   Macaroni and cheese

The above quick menu suggestions might include:

1. *Chicken chow mein:* canned chicken and broth, Chinese vegetables, water chestnuts, mushrooms, Chinese fried noodles, quick rice, and soy sauce. The *chicken and dumplings* need the canned chicken and broth and biscuit mix. Serve with cranberry sauce and green vegetables. A fruit salad completes either meal . . . all from the pantry.

2. *Salmon loaf:* canned pink or red salmon, green olives, other relishes, and slaw if you have cabbage; potatoes to bake with the loaf. Serve with yellow or green vegetables and pineapple/mandarin orange sections for a tart dessert.

3. *Spaghetti:* canned or your own frozen spaghetti sauce with meat, Parmesan cheese, thin pasta, and lots of green salad. The canned might not be as good as homemade but can be improved with additional seasonings and mushrooms. Children like it. Brownies and ice cream from the freezer can be a good finish.

4. *Ham and sweet potatoes:* This is a good oven meal. A canned ham, usually kept refrigerated, can be put in the oven to brown, topped with your quick mustard/brown sugar sauce. Meanwhile, make a sweet potato casserole with canned sweet potatoes and your other favorite seasonings. Next, make a pineapple upside-down cake from a mix to bake with the ham and sweet potatoes. Serve this meal with a variety of relishes and any green vegetable.

5. *Macaroni and cheese:* Grated cheddar cheese (frozen

or fresh), macaroni pasta, milk. While baking toss a quick salad and cook a green vegetable. A quickset berry gelatin or instant chocolate pudding would add a contrast in color.

The pantry should include canned fruits for salads or desserts; pineapple and cake mix for cake; pineapple and pear halves for cheese/fruit salads; and a variety of canned vegetables. Three varieties of canned beans with onions and a vinegar dressing make a quick, tart salad.

On your shelves have boxes of pizza and brownie mix plus any other mixes your family might favor. Cans of applesauce, pickled beets, relishes, and other accompaniments can help in any pinch and are usually liked by most people.

As you have gathered, our experiences and preferences tend to make us a bit more cautious regarding emergency meals. Thus, we've learned these ways to meet those challenges head on. There really is a satisfaction in being able to face these situations with poise . . . yes, even fun. That is what our concept of "capers" implies . . . lightheartedly rejoicing at the expected and the unexpected. What peace!

8
Supermarket Savvy

We think we've solved the problem of how to afford to entertain! Surveys show that almost every family can save between 10 and 20 percent on its food budget by careful management and wise shopping. If so, that is sufficient to "fund our fun."

The two of us looked at our own habits. Even as home economists who shop carefully, we have to admit that we too could sharpen our marketing practices. Who doesn't want more gold for the good times as well as the daily morsels?

"What would happen," Marge speculated, "if a supermarket advertised that on a certain day they would give away 'golden keys' guaranteed to save the holder 10 to 20 percent on all future food bills?"

We decided that a mob would storm the entire area the night before . . . waiting for the doors to fling open: not the usual mob scene, but some people in business suits, senior citizens, smartly dressed women, and couples with children —all clamoring for their keys.

Being the realists that we are, we also figured that when the mob discovered that the "golden keys" were simply rules for wise shopping, they would probably riot in a rage and try to lynch the manager for misleading them.

Yet these keys to wise shopping are worth their weight in gold—week after week. No doubt you already use many of them regularly. Read to check for the others which will help you save 10 percent or more on your food costs.

Keys to Shopping Savings

1. Don't drive all over town to save a few cents here and there. Time and fuel are money too. Decide on your favorite one or two markets and shop only there. The competition is so keen they'll never be far out of line.

2. Be aware that small stores with home delivery, charge accounts, and extra services must charge to cover these costs.

3. Review your storage techniques—for example, don't pay good money to run a freezer to store things which are always available at the same price. One loaf of bread is fine, but why freeze a dozen and not have the space for a company meal or seasonal savings? Or before you snap up a bulk bargain, be sure that you have adequate storage space.

4. Find the time you can shop when the produce is freshest and the store is least crowded (usually early in the day).

5. Never shop when you are hungry. You buy too much junk food you can eat in the car, and you also overspend.

6. Keep a continuous shopping list and add items as they run low to save on "crisis" trips.

7. Menus should be planned weekly at home while checking the pantry, the refrigerator, and the newspaper ads for coupons and specials. From the menus, a grocery list should be made.

8. After making the menu, also check cupboards for staples, replacements for what you've used from your emergency shelf, spices needed, cleaning supplies, and sundries.

Forgetting just one thing is costly in terms of time, energy, and money for an extra trip to the market.

9. Check the newspaper ads for "loss leaders." These are items sold at or below cost to entice you to come to that store. If it is something you use regularly, consider stocking up. Write the sale price on your list.

10. Usually the newspaper ad will feature one meat, fish, or poultry as a loss leader. If you have a freezer, stock up on that one protein source. Over a month's time, you should have a variety of meat, all at very low prices. Then vary your meals based on that treasured cache. You'll have the nucleus for some delightful entertainment events.

11.Try never to shop with kids. If you need to be told why, you don't have any yet!

12. Buy meat by cost per serving—not cost per pound. Spare ribs at $1.98 per pound are more expensive than a sirloin tip roast at $4.00 per pound. The ribs are $1.98 per serving while the roast is $1.00.

13. Be aware of the sales techniques used by the supermarkets, but don't be mislead by them. Supermarket savvy means you have power. You're in command. But be courteous and fair, and practice the "golden rule" in supermarket shopping as well as all other business interactions.

14. Never overbuy perishable items. Learn how to select prime fruits and vegetables.

15. Be adventuresome. At least once a month, try the smallest quantity of a food you've never eaten or prepared. You will discover some new favorites and won't get in a rut. Then later, some of these foods may be part of your entertainment fare . . . a fun experience for all to share.

16. Some packages or bottles have odd shapes. Check weight or volume to compare value. Smart shopping means you use your head to save your wallet.

17. Check expiration dates on milk, dairy products, cold cuts, eggs, bakery goods, etc., and buy the freshest possible.

18. Buy larger eggs if the difference in price is ten cents or less. Buy smaller if the price difference is more than ten cents. And there is no difference in quality or nutrition between brown and white eggs.

19. Become a label reader. "Grape drink" is 10 percent juice and 90 percent water and sugar. All words ending in "ose" should be spelled s-u-g-a-r. If sodium is a problem in your family, look for it on the ingredient list and avoid that food. The label lists every ingredient in order by weight.

20. Check the unit pricing if your supermarket uses this system. It saves you from calculating whether the large or small size or an item is the best buy.

21. Be alert at checkout. More errors are made at grocery checkouts than in any form of retailing—20 percent of all tickets have a mistake. Particularly watch specials which may not be marked on the package. Ask your cashier how to handle the coupons before beginning. Check your noted special prices as they are rung up. Visiting with checkers or others at this time can be costly.

22. Ask for a rain check if the store is out of an advertised special. They are required by law to give you one.

23. Go directly home and properly store food. This means washing most fresh vegetables and storing airtight in the refrigerator, repackaging and freezing meat into one-meal portions, washing and refrigerating most fruit, and getting ice cream in the freezer immediately. Don't waste the quality you've bought.

24. Check your register total at home for amounts charged as you put away the groceries. Circle a questionable amount and inquire about it.

25. Return merchandise that is not satisfactory for some

reason. Be fair, and you can expect management to be. Keep your receipts/tapes for a refund, but be considerate regarding the timing—the Friday PM rush hour is not the ideal time.

26. Lastly, if you use coupons, check purchase against coupon as you select the product. Or if you plan to send for refunds, be organized about it. You must be painstakingly diligent to make refunds or coupons worth your time and effort.

More Pocketbook Power

What a list! And it could go on. No doubt you have a favorite savings tip we haven't even mentioned. After all, the 19 to 30 percent of our income which we spend on food is for most of us the largest chunk of discretionary money we handle. That's why we sometimes hear someone say, "I bought it out of the grocery money." The mortgage payment is a fixed amount, but if we need some extra dollars, sometimes we can eat a few more meals of beans or macaroni and cheese and channel our cash to the other need.

If we know the elements of good nutrition, we can meet our physical needs for food with a more modest expenditure. The pleasure of eating and our passion for certain foods play a significant role along with basic nutrition in determining how vital food is in our lives and how much we shall spend for it.

Contemporary life-styles include eating out more, which takes an increasingly large slice of the family's food money, especially in dual career homes. Before we condemn the practice which costs double dollars, we need to realize that all of our resources—including time—are limited. Only you can decide what is best for you in the various transitions of your life.

At the supermarket, the management with 15,000-plus items for sale is depending on high-volume sales at a stark one half of one percent profit to make the store's big bucks. Top management is backed by every possible bit of marketing research a national chain can buy, and it knows consumers (that's us) right down to whether we have a shopping list. When we enter the store, we are under the influence of a variety of carefully researched sales techniques, and we gain power when we understand what they are.

To begin with, to encourage our coming to their store, they make shopping there a pleasant experience. Adequate parking, air conditioning, skillful lighting, a clean store, colorful displays, soft music, wide aisles, numerous checkout cashiers, and the smell of fresh bakery goods enhance the chore.

We were amazed to learn that only about 10 percent of those of us who come to shop are prepared to save money by making a list of what we need to buy and sticking to it. It is estimated that up to three fourths of all supermarket purchases are impulse decisions.

Trade Secrets

Some of the marketing techniques used to tempt us to leave our hard-earned bucks in the store include:

• Luscious fresh produce—a high profit/high loss item —is beautifully arranged just as we begin our tour of the store. We still feel in control of our money, and it's easier to tempt us to overbuy or buy the more exotic items.

• Special displays at the end of aisles—often dumped in baskets—look like specials, and the sale of these slow-moving or new items doubles, even when the price is identical to the shelf price.

- High-cost brands are placed near eye level. We can save 10 percent by checking the brand near the floor or on the top shelf.
- Generic brands, which are just as desirable in many recipes, are placed away from name brands and store brands, so prices are harder to compare.
- Two for odd cents causes most of us to buy the second item whether or not we have any plans for using it.
- Meat is arranged across the back of the store to tempt us at the foot of every aisle.
- Beware of the store that uses pink lights over the meat and pink plastic wraps for tomatoes to make the food look better than it is.
- Any wrapped food is placed on the tray to show its best side. In other words, for meat, the bony or fat side is down.
- One staple per aisle is the golden rule, with milk in the far back corner. That way, when we pop in for a few staple items, we are tempted by the endless other items we must pass. The chances are we'll pick up one or two items we didn't plan.
- "Piggybacking" or "hitchhiking" is deliberate and legal for management but near lethal for the consumer. Let's say we come to buy the ice cream special, and there beside it are displays of chopped nuts, maraschino cherries, and luscious syrups in five flavors. What do we buy? Right! And the store makes a big profit.
- Silent salesmen on every aisle appeal to our impulses with nonfood items—brushes by the barbecue sauce, bottle openers at the soft drink counter, etc. These items usually cost more when purchased in a supermarket.
- Budget breakers line the checkout counter. We are offered magazines, candy, gum, batteries, and breath mints

that TV tells us we need. The extra nonfood items strike a fatal blow to our planned thrift.

Can you relate to this enticing conspiracy? Management does its job almost to perfection and is to be commended, but our role as consumers is to be equally astute in providing for our household's needs with a minimum expenditure. Although we don't have a bankroll to spend on research, we can share insights and techniques to help restore equilibrium to our food budgets.

The winner is the one who understands best how the system works and uses that knowledge to his or her own advantage. Anyone can be a winner.

One Last Thought

In the United States the percentage of our incomes which we spend for food is far less than most other people of the world spend for their food. We are blessed with clean, safe supermarkets, with the enviable productivity of our agriculture and food networks, and we enjoy the world's greatest variety and abundance. Truly, we should be thankful for our daily bread!

9
Nutrition Notes:
The Abundant Life

Christians have been given the abundant life. Rather than a spiritual application, let's make a physical application of that priceless promise. Every day of our lives we bear the evidence of our nutritional status. Only if we are well nourished do we have a chance of being vibrantly alive. Good nutrition contributes to our having boundless energy; strong, firm muscles; bright and clear eyes; glowing skin; good appetite; freedom from disease; desirable weight; and beautiful hair, nails, and teeth.

To achieve this abundant physical status in today's hectic world may be both easier and harder than it was for our grandparents. We have to plan more deliberately to get plenty of fresh air and exercise. We may experience more sophisticated stressors, making relaxation more difficult. We may have an ample year-round food supply which at the same time probably is too low in fiber and too high in sugar, sodium, and cholesterol. A twentieth-century paradox!

In the last decade or two Americans have become very health conscious. Ten billion dollars a year are spent on health club and spa memberships, exercise clothing and equipment, and diet foods, books, and pills. Joggers and cyclists abound. Physical fitness is "in," and industry, business, and government all play significant roles in promotion and education. Health and nutrition education is big business.

Nutrition education in itself is positive, yet the amount of misinformation which floods the market annually is frightening. New books which tout food fads are published monthly. Not only is the quantity of information confusing, but so much of it is poorly researched and has only a profit motive. If there is a product for sale, be skeptical. No "quick fix" can ever replace the self-discipline needed to moderate life habits and bring long-range desired changes. While millions of dollars are spent on special foods, clothing, and equipment, not one penny is required beyond basic food to be adequately nourished, exercised, and rested.

Manna in the Marketplace?

Another spin-off of our awareness of the importance of good health is the proliferation of "health food" stores. They charge at least 10 percent more for foods which are usually available in a supermarket and up to 40 percent more for those foods not easily found. Many such health food stores promote "organically grown" produce and such products as fructose and sea salt which are priced much higher than regular produce, sugar, and salt. The misinformed refuse to believe that fructose really is a sugar like sucrose, maltose, dextrose, and all the "ose" family, including honey, molasses, High Fructose Cane Sugar (H.F.C.S.), and cane syrup. The misinformed believe the unrefined sea salt is somehow better for their bodies than plain table salt. But the minute traces of other nutrients in honey or sea salt are so small as to be totally insignificant and are of no consequence except to the budget!

Go ahead and buy from the health food stores if you choose, but do so from a knowledge base confirmed by research. You can count on the government's delivery system of latest research findings through the United States Department of Agriculture (U.S.D.A.), the U. S. Department of Health, Education and Welfare, and major medical groups. These are generally the only groups conducting ongoing in-depth research which requires millions of dollars annually. Admittedly the U. S. government isn't perfect, but neither are the private manufacturers.

Fearfully and Wonderfully Made

We have often heard it said that someone is a "bundle of nerves." That really isn't true, of course, but it could accurately be said that all of us are "bundles of chemicals." Everything on earth—animal, vegetable, or mineral—is chemical. Every cell in our body is made up of chemical bonds, and everything we eat or drink is a mixture of chemicals. So "chemicals" are not necessarily harmful to us. Some are necessary on a regular basis for life.

One type of the chemicals we eat or drink is called vitamins, and each vitamin has a specific job to do. Without it we develop one of the deficiency diseases now almost extinct in this northern hemisphere. Our vitamin problem here in North America is not a lack of what we need but the confusion caused by misinformation about "natural" versus "synthetic" vitamins, amounts required, and what foods contain them.

In a nutshell, our bodies cannot distinguish between vitamins and minerals from a natural source, such as a food, and vitamins and minerals synthesized in a laboratory. Therefore, a unit of Vitamin A acts exactly the same in our bodies whether we get it from a carrot or from a vitamin tablet. In fact, if we do get it from a vitamin tablet, it should be the least expensive one we can buy, for the law requires the manufacturer to meet specific criteria and the vitamins are identical.

Research has established how many units of each known vitamin and mineral we need every day if our health is normal. These amounts are called Recommended Daily Allowance, or R.D.A.'s. Because they would be very difficult for us to remember or figure, the U.S.D.A. has categorized foods in four groups, with a fifth group that furnishes mostly calories. When we eat the recommended servings of each group daily, we are assured of being well nourished. At the end of this chapter is the U.S.D.A.'s listing of these groups with the number of servings and serving sizes. Variety assures us of all our needs.

Frequently we hear claims that megadoses of certain vitamins prevent colds or acne or other diseases. We would caution you that unless your physician prescribes for you, you should not take megadoses of anything. If you eat a balanced diet with a variety of foods, you don't need any supplementary vitamins at all. When your body has 100 percent of what it can use on any day, it cannot use more. If there is an excess of vitamins, they have to be stored or disposed of in some way. That puts a strain on the kidneys if the vitamins are water soluble. If the vitamins are fat soluble, they are stored in body fat. They can become toxic when the amount is excessive.

Another group of nutrients our body needs is minerals. Iron, calcium, phosphorus, zinc, and others are necessary for life.

One of the food groups—milk and milk products—is mainly for the purpose of furnishing calcium, which we now know is needed by the body as long as we live. Many adults quit drinking milk and during their adult years they really are calcium deficient. When the body needs calcium for normal nerve transmission or blood clotting, it robs the bones and teeth to meet its need. The bones in turn become porous and very fragile and develop a condition known as osteoporosis.

Happily for all of us who are not specialists in nutrition, the research has been done for us by those who are. Again, we should follow the R.D.A.'s for a dietary pattern.

Food Categories

Nutritionally speaking, all foods are either carbohydrates (starches or sugars), protein, or fat. Carbohydrates are plant in origin. Vegetables start out as sugars and, as they ripen, turn into starches. Fruits, on the other hand, are starches that change into sugars as they mature. Carbohydrates, because of their chemical composition, are easily digested and absorbed by the body. Foods high in carbohydrates carry vitamins, minerals, and fiber as well as furnishing much of the energy or fuel the body needs.

Proteins are made up of twenty-two amino acids and complete proteins are animal in origin. Protein is necessary for us to build and repair our body tissue. Fourteen of the amino acids can be manufactured by the body from other foods, but eight of them must be eaten if the body is to have them.

Some plants are good sources of amino acids and are called "incomplete proteins." If the plants which complement each other are eaten at the same meal so that they digest together, the amino acids which are present form protein. The body is then as well nourished as if meat had been consumed. The rule of thumb is to eat a whole grain product with a legume (whatever grows in a pod). This would include:

- a peanut butter sandwich made with whole wheat bread
- red beans over brown rice (Hoppin' John)
- soup beans and cornbread

Fats are the third big category into which all foods fit, and they come from both plants and animals. Generally speaking, animal fats are saturated and are high in cholesterol. These fats are solid at room temperature. Three vegetable fats which are highly saturated are coconut and palm oils (the two big nuts!) and cocoa butter found in chocolate. Otherwise vegetable oils are generally low in saturated fats and have no cholesterol, which makes them much healthier to eat than animal fats.

Fats are not just a problem because of weight control. The overconsumption of fats is related to increased risks of heart disease, high blood pressure, some cancers, diabetes, and other health breakdowns.

Giants in the Land

How can we win in this battle for optimum health and nutritional status? We can practice what we already know, such as using a good margarine instead of that butter we dearly love, and read labels to ensure that neither coconut nor palm oil is listed among the first ingredients. We can limit organ meats, trim the visible fat from meat, and skin chicken before cooking. We can choose not to fry foods and not to use fat meat to season vegetables. We can eat more fish and chicken, less beef, pork, and lamb. We can refrigerate soups, sauces, and meat stock before using in order to skim off and discard the hardened fat which rises to the top. These precautions may be lifesaving for the average American, who gets 41 percent of his calories from fat when 30 percent would be ideal. There is enough fat marbled through lean meat and found naturally in other foods to give us all we need.

More Giants

Whole milk is also a rich source of saturated fat. Every adult needs the other nutrients in milk or milk products, but we don't need the fat in cream. By law, the fat-soluble Vitamin A from the cream is put back into 2 percent and skim milk so we get it plus the advantages of all the minerals and protein without the calories and saturated fat. If we use uncreamed cottage cheese, low-fat cheeses, and a good grade of margarine and reduced fat milk, our fat level from the milk group can be kept within bounds.

Eggs are the other animal product we all eat regularly. The yolk is very fatty and high in cholesterol. Egg whites have no fat at all and can be safely eaten to your heart's delight.

Calories

Now all foods contain fuel or energy that our bodies must have. The energy is measured in calories. If we don't take in enough fuel for our needs, our body uses some previously stored as body fat, and we lose weight. If we eat more calories than we use, our very efficient body stores it for further use. But in North America, we seldom know hunger. Consequently obesity is the number one nutritional problem, especially in the United States. We will deal with this topic in the following chapter on weight control.

All foods do not contain the same amount of energy. By categories it goes like this:

4 calories/gram in carbohydrates
4 calories/gram in proteins

9 calories/gram in fats

It becomes obvious how a person who consumes large amounts of fat, which is in the Fifth Food Group with almost no nutrients, can weigh enough or actually be obese and still be malnourished. Here is another nutritional paradox!

Nutritionally it is to our advantage to cut down on the concentrated calories of fats and sweets, which tend to be empty of other nutrients. Most of us are lacking complex carbohydrates—such as beans, peas, nuts, seeds, unpeeled fruits, vegetables, and whole grain products—which contain many essential nutrients in addition to calories. These complex carbohydrates are also high in fiber. Fiber is the part of plants which is neither digested nor absorbed but adds bulk to the diet and decreases chronic constipation. Fiber also helps in regulating the diets of diabetics, helps prevent obesity, and decreases the risk of colon cancer.

Sweet Tooth Gone Wild

There are two other common food ingredients besides animal fats we should deliberately curtail for maximum health: sugar and sodium. Our sugar intake in the U. S. is 130 pounds per person per year, up from 4 pounds in Napoleon's time when the lowly sugar beet's potential was discovered. Oh, how we love sugar! Processors of food add sugar to almost everything—to vegetables, salad dressings, and baby food, where it certainly is not needed, just to please the public's sweet tooth and to surreptitiously increase sales. Why else is sugar added to peanut butter? We should avidly read labels to look for the "ose" family if we are to avoid tooth decay and obesity. By listing each kind of sugar separately, the manufacturer is often able to avoid listing sugar as the first (and weightiest) ingredient in his product.

Parents Beware

Parents should be aware that children between the ages of 5 and 11 in the U. S. eat an average of 2/3 cup of sugar every day. If we get 24 percent of our calories from sugar and 41 percent of our calories from fat, both of which are empty calories with no other nutritional value, that only leaves 35 percent of our calories to furnish 100 percent of our nutrition—impossible!

Since only 6 percent of our sugar intake occurs naturally in fruits and other foods, and only 33 percent is added to foods in the home, we quickly see that the more we can cut back on processed foods and prepare our own foods, the more sugar and sodium we can avoid. Hopefully parents will become aware of the hazards and begin to help their children break the food habits which lead to this cycle of bondage.

Salt Out of Control

Sodium or salt, which is sodium chloride, is the third health threat along with fats and sugar in our diets. Almost daily for our whole lifetime we eat three to four times as much sodium as we need. Since sodium is a major factor in high blood pressure, is it any wonder we have about 15 percent of our adults suffering from this life threat?

It is a mistake to think that foods must taste salty to be high in sodium. Seventy percent of our sodium intake may be "hidden" in naturally occurring foods or added to commercially prepared foods such as soft drinks, many antacids and medications, baking soda, baking powder, lunchmeats, pickled foods, and monosodium glutamate (MSG). Ten to thirty percent of our sodium comes from salt added at the table or cooking at home.

It is almost unbelievable how processing increases the sodium content of food. For instance, a cucumber has 5 mg. of sodium but a dill pickle has 928 mg. One cup of fresh peas has 2 mg. of sodium, but one cup of caanned peas has 493 mg. Let's return to fresh or frozen food choices if we can or pour off the liquid and rinse canned vegetables for 1 minute under running water, which will reduce the sodium content over 80 percent.

Besides using fewer processed foods, we need to learn to: avoid salty foods; enjoy the unsalted flavors of foods; read labels; cook with less salt; and take the salt shaker off the table. Use herbs and spices and especially lemons to flavor foods.

Above all, avoid salt substitutes unless your physician prescribes them. They substitute potassium chloride for sodium chloride aand an excess of either is not good.

Food Additives

And now hear the last issue which is so complex as to defy a simple solution. A stormy debate swirls around the issue of food additives. Experts disagree, new research constantly changes what is accepted as safe, long-term results are not yet in, and consumers are demanding more convenience, year-round availability, and exotic foods.

A Parable

Thousands of years ago in the earliest time of man when a big kill was made, the entire clan helped devour it. Perhaps there was a "fast" until the next available food to share, but between the big animal kills, individuals gathered edible plants and snared the tiny creatures.

The time came in ancient Egypt when those who lived there, as well as their neighbors, practiced the art of salting foods and using vinegar to preserve foods and ward off decay. They also knew how to store grain in dry places to prevent mold and spoilage, but everywhere obtaining the family's food was a daily chore that almost consumed them.

But life-styles changed, even then. Years passed and gradually people in another land began to associate their diseases such as rickets, pellagra, goiter, and beri-beri with improper foodstuff. Finally the sovereign decreed that Vitamin D be added to milk, Vitamin A to margarine, iodine to salt, and B Vitamins to bread and flours. Then the treacherous diseases almost disappeared in the countries where the rulers cared enough to enforce the decrees.

Alas, alas! Progress began to rampage through an increasingly technological world. Additives were put into foods to maintain freshness or to make them look more palatable and beautiful. Later nitrates and nitrites were added to meat to keep it from spoiling. The controversy still rages regarding the safety of each, but they are considered safe if done properly and under the sovereign's specific controls.

Time passed, yet modern man yearned for more and more. Not only did he want to enrich diets, replace ingredients lost in processing, and preserve freshness and safety, but he also wanted to have better products. He wanted homogenized peanut butter as opposed to the oil and layer of peanut "cement" and other amenities.

Man wanted to eat foods grown all over the world. The situation may be almost a "Babel" now, and man has begun to ask whether there is a limit to what processors of food can do and whether there is a limit to what they should do. Thus the controversy continues.

Turn Back the Clock?

But this parable doesn't end. Almost 98 percent by weight of all additives used are sugar, salt and corn syrup, plus citric acid, soda, vegetable coloring, mustard, and pepper. Should we turn back the clock?

With our life-styles, we can't turn back the clock. We treasure all the variety of food available to us year-round. We won't tolerate botulism and other diseases brought on by contaminated foods—which were common prior to the turn of the century.

While we can't turn back the clock, we can:

1. Learn about additives. Read labels as if your life depended on it (it may). Contact your nearest Food and Drug Administration (F.D.A.) office listed in the telephone directory under U. S. Department of Health, Education and Welfare. Ask questions.

2. Choose wisely for your family, but be tolerant of those who choose differently.

3. Let your Legislators and the manufacturers know what you do and do not want in food.

Reminder

Are you still with us after this mini crash course in nutrition? In case you got discouraged about ever achieving a more healthful food pattern for yourself, your family, and guests, let us encourage you to make just one change at a time. When you feel comfortable with that change, choose the next area needing changing and work on it. Your guests will appreciate any invitation to eat and fellowship in your home. So guests, who only eat with you occasionally, are not of major concern in your nutrition planning. Improving

your nutrition is the gift you give yourself and those who
live with you. Claim and pass on your abundant life!

Dietary Guidelines for Americans

1. Eat a variety of foods.
2. Maintain desirable weight.
3. Avoid too much fat, saturated fat, and cholesterol.
4. Eat foods with adequate starch and fiber.
5. Avoid too much sugar.
6. Avoid too much sodium.

The Hassle-Free Daily Food Guide

Vegetable-Fruit Group (4 servings daily)
1 serving is:

1/2 cup	**an orange**
a small salad	**1/2 cantaloupe**
a medium-sized potato	**1/2 grapefruit**

Have citrus fruit, melon, berries, or tomatoes daily and a
dark-green or dark-yellow vegetable frequently. For a good
source of fiber, eat unpeeled fruits and vegetables and fruits
with edible seeds—berries or grapes.

Bread-Cereal Group (4 servings daily)
1 serving is:

1 slice bread	**1 ounce ready-to eat cereal**
1/2 to 3/4 cup cooked cereal or pasta	

Choose whole-grain products often.

Milk-Cheese Group (2 to 4 servings daily)

Servings: *1 serving is:*

Adults—2   1 cup milk or yogurt
Children under 9 years old—2-3   1 1/3 ounces cheddar or swiss
Children 9-12 years old   cheese
   and pregnant women—3   2 ounces processed cheese food
Teens and nursing mothers—4   1 1/2 cups ice cream or ice milk
                                    2 cups cottage cheese

Skim, nonfat, and lowfat milk and milk products provide calcium and keep fat intake down.

Meat and Poultry, Fish and Beans Group (2 servings daily)

1/2 serving is:

1 to 1 1/2 ounces lean,   2 tablespoons peanut butter
   boneless, cooked meat,   1/4 to 1/2 cup nuts, sesame or
   poultry, or fish   sunflower seeds
1 egg
1/2 to 3/4 cup cooked dry beans,
   peas, lentils, or soybeans

Poultry and fish have less fat content than red meats.

Fats-Sweets Group

Caution: These foods provide calories but few nutrients.

10
Simplicity Satisfies

Simple is classic in every area of our lives. Nowhere is it more appreciated than in the area of foods.

We have suggested that one-dish meals might be the answer to many family meals as well as entertaining events. Most of us have special one-dish or casserole recipes which are favorites with family and friends. Perhaps we should, each on our own, develop four or five of these specialties and plan more meals around them. With the addition of a salad and dessert, little more is needed. And all these can be done ahead of time.

The reasons for simple, do-ahead meals are obvious . . . no last-minute trauma; you choose your best time to do the work; these meals usually hold well and carry well if need be. The option of doubling or tripling the recipe gives another advantage often overlooked. Leftovers (especially meat) can be fully utilized in casseroles.

Casseroles

We use the term *casserole* rather loosely. To us it is any food which is made ahead and combined in one dish . . . usually served hot. Even chili or soup falls in this category.

Some persons feel the casserole or simple one-dish meal

is family fare but never to be served to guests. Nonsense! Simple one-dish meals rate high . . . whether they are served indoors or on the patio. By the way, dining rooms can have a chilling effect on some people. Perhaps a simple food and setting would help bridge the gap between the summer cookout and the elegance of fine china, crystal, and linen. Whatever, family and company needs are identical; family doesn't always have to let it all hang out, and company doesn't always have to get the special treatment—both need nourishment and fellowship. Either may need the red carpet treatment and candelight or to be completely relaxed and comfortable, such as munching popcorn by a crackling fire.

Some of our favorite casseroles include ethnic dishes as well as the traditional, such as:

> Lasagna, chili, "Hoppin John," ham/scalloped potatoes; tamale pie, a variety of stews—lamb, beef, chicken; a variety of quiches, cabbage, rolls, tuna bake; crab casserole, turkey tetrazzini, pot pies, endless chicken casseroles, beef stroganoff, moussaka, burgoo; goulash, pastas, and a variety of Oriental dishes; corned beef, cabbage, potatoes, and carrots.

Many of these dishes are perfect for the slow cooker or the microwave as well as the conventional oven or range.

In addition to casseroles containing meat, there are many recipes of main dishes containing other proteins. Not only vegetarians love these, but most of the rest of us enjoy them for a change. Usually a combination of whole grains, legumes, eggs, and cheese substitute for the meat to make a satisfying main dish. As with any casserole, these are do-ahead meals too. The fun is in the heating and eating, not necessarily in the preparation. Remember when adding cheese as a topping, do it the last few minutes of baking time to prevent the cheese from becoming hard.

Many vegetables make good casserole combinations and thus share in the do-ahead, enjoy-later category. If you haven't tried these, develop your own specialties and use when planning an oven meal or baking a dessert or bread. Often a vegetable that is not liked when served plain (squash or eggplant) is enjoyed in a casserole.

Cobblers, fruit crisps, pudding cakes, and bread puddings are among other do-ahead goodies. Any one-dish warm dessert will win praise in your home. Peruse your cookbooks again for ideas for the meat, pasta, vegetable, or dessert casseroles. You might be challenged in a new way for all your meal planning. The following sections will add some specific suggestions for simplicity in meals.

Soups and Stews

There are basically two types of soups . . . those with a milk or white sauce base and those with a broth or juice base. For starters, each of us should master a thin white sauce. Then the sky is the limit for such delicious concoctions as: Cheddar cheese soup, chicken soups, corn chowder, cream of anything soup, potato soup, mushroom soup, oyster stew, and fresh tomato soup.

Be sure not to boil or put a cover on a milk-based soup as it will cause it to curdle. Also with homemade tomato soup, heat the tomatoes to near boiling and add slowly to the hot milk base. Thus the acid is neutralized slowly and is not likely to curdle.

Learn to make soup stock from meat and bones or use the canned bouillon or consommé. The powdered or cubed bouillon contains much more sodium, and we prefer the homemade or canned anyway. Often some grain or starch (barley, macaroni, rice, dumplings, or legumes) is added to a hearty soup.

One of our favorite stock-based soups is the French onion soup, topped with a slice of French bread and parmesan cheese. Some other stock or meat-based soups include chicken, vegetable/beef, borscht, split pea, fish chowders, and bean soup. One of the most popular dishes in the U. S. Senate cafeteria is the bean soup, and it really is easily made but takes a long time to cook. Many people prefer bean soup served with corn bread.

Certain other soups traditionally require crackers, and oyster stew calls for oyster crackers. Although soups are good anytime, cold weather seems to enhance a hearty, hot soup. Add a hot bread such as corn bread, cheesy muffins, French bread, dark grain bread, or popcorn. With home-made chili, consider serving spicy Mexican corn bread.

Even in warm weather lighter soups are tasty. Gazpacho or the cold vegetable soups hit the spot then. After a cooking binge or when garden vegetables are in their glory, try making "sink" soup (everything but the kitchen sink) for eating and for freezing. Soups are economical, nutritious, and delicious. What more can we ask? And we've said before, cook a recipe for now and some for the freezer. Later, you will be grateful.

Some things to remember about cooking soups are: If made with meats, chill the broth and skim off the hardened fat. Potatoes are not good frozen, so add to soup when you are planning to serve it. Be light with seasonings; it is easy to get heavy handed. Seasonings can either be added at the last minute or left for each person do his or her own thing. If soup tastes too salty, add a potato or vegetable juice (such as tomato). If a puree of vegetables is needed, lift cooked vegetables out of the broth and puree in blender or processor. Then return to the base. In the winter months, buy frozen mixed vegetables to add to the soup or stew late in the cooking process. One gets corn, beans, peas, etc., to add color to the usual carrots, potatoes, and onions always in the pantry or fridge.

One last thing: Use garnishes when appropriate, such as cheeses, croutons, sour cream, chopped parsley, green onions, lemon slices, or sunflower seeds. Besides the eye appeal, these add taste, texture, and zest.

Now about stews: Perhaps stews could be defined as simply thick soups, with lots of chunks of meat? There isn't the variety of stew recipes that there is for soups, but there really is something for everyone.

There is a basic stew made from cubed meat, browned, with onions, seasonings, and liquid. This can be made in quantity and frozen in meal-size containers. When using, the variations include:

All-time favorite: Add to basic mixture peas, carrots, seaonings, flour, and toppings (biscuits, dumplings, or whipped potatoes).

Mexican: Add to basic mixture tomatoes and vegetables such as corn, limas, and a bit of hot sauce.

Sweet/sour: Add to basic mixture onions, green pepper strips, carrot strips, tomato sauce, vinegar, brown sugar or molasses, and seasonings such as soy sauce or chili powder.

Beef stew and fruit: Add to basic mixture sweet potatoes, onions, green peppers, corn, zucchini, and peaches or apricots (lean pork could be substituted for beef here).

Hungarian Goulash: Add equal amounts of veal or pork to basic mixture, then add onions, sour cream, and seasonings.

Five-hour stew: Add to basic mixture carrots, onions,

potatoes, a can of tomato soup or tomatoes or mixed vegetable juices, water, a small amount of vinegar or pickle juice,
seasonings, and tapioca. Bake for five hours at 250-275 degrees.

Meats other than beef can be used, such as veal or lamb.
Lamb stew is popular in many regions and is delicious. One
favorite is lamb and lentil stew with chicken broth as a base,
onions, celery, and lentils.

Two other regional specialties are Brunswick stew and
Polish stew. To the chicken add tomatoes, limas, corn, pork
tenderloin, potatoes, and seasonings. In the Polish stew use
Kielbasa sausage, vegetables, water, and seasonings. Add
cabbage when almost done. To dispel the odor when cooking with cabbage or brussel sprouts, add celery. It does help.

Things to remember about stews are:

—Stews need some type of thickening (tapioca, flour, or
pasta).

—Stews are usually cooked slow and low with a cover.
Add green vegetables such as peas in the latter stage of
cooking.

—The addition of sour cream or tomato sauce gives a
creamy sauerbraten flavor. These items are usually added
late in the cooking process.

—Less tender meat cuts may be used, but this calls for
added time and/or a tenderizing agent (vinegar, tomatoes)
and perhaps more liquid.

—Meats are browned or precooked. There must be a
gravy whether you make it, it develops in the cooking process with the liquids, or you add some type of convenience
product.

—You can be as creative as you wish with vegetables and
seasonings and make your stew a truly individual dish.

Any of the stews are good with green salads or a fruity

salad. We like stewed apricots, toasted French bread slices (or corn sticks), and a light dessert with most stews. Stews are usually soft, hot, chunky, and meaty; so tart, fruity, cold, and crunchy accompaniments seem to be in order.

If you have a slow cooker, the recipe book should abound with stew suggestions. Use your imagination to develop these and other crowd pleasers.

With both soups and stews, most of the European and Middle Eastern cooks excel in these dishes and would put most of us in North America to shame. Whether this is because the cooks were forced to be ingenious over the years because of a scarcity of meat or because they simply didn't have all the choices in cooking methods and equipment which we have available is just a guess. But the canned variety familiar to most of us today is a poor substitute for glorious homemade soups and stews. Maybe these cooks could teach us something about entertaining with simplicity.

Managing Meats, Poultry, Fish, and Seafood

Most of us start planning a menu around a protein source. It is our largest expenditure for food, and certain foods seem to "go" with certain meats, poultry, or fish. The meat even dictates how special a meal might be considered.

In our chapter on Supermarket Savvy, we encouraged you to shop for the loss leader many supermarkets offer weekly in their meat departments. If you do buy sirloin-tip roasts or chicken pieces or whatever when they are on sale, be aware that all meats must be rewrapped for the freezer. The store packaging is temporary and will not prevent dehydration. You also will want to trim, wrap, and label in one-meal portions your meats or chicken for freezing.

If you are one of those persons who has her own farm

animals or can buy a standing half from a friend, you will
have your dressed meat cut and packaged for the freezer
to your specifications, then labeled and frozen to perfection. However, before deciding on bulk purchases, be sure
your freezer space is adequate. One cubic feet of space will
hold 35-40 pounds of wrapped meat, less if the packages are
odd shaped.

You will also need to be able to use the meat while it is
in prime condition. Beef and lamb store longer than pork.
Recommended storage times at 0 degrees F are:

 Beef and lamb roasts and chops: 8-12 months
 Beef and lamb ground: 3-4 months
 Pork roast and chops: 4-8 months
 Ground pork: 1-3 months
 Cured meat: 1-3 months

A consumer needs to recognize cuts of meat and to be
able to use the appropriate cooking method. Besides cooking with moist heat, the less tender cuts can be tenderized
by scoring, pounding, grinding, or marinating with an acid
such as vinegar or lemon juice. Tenderizing enzymes also
can be purchased. The tender cuts need no special help and
are usually grilled, broiled, panbroiled, roasted, or fried.

Whatever the cut of beef—or meat—you are cooking,
turn down the heat. Low heat is the secret of both successful and money-saving meat cookery. Avoid high tempera-
tures and overcooking that shrink a roast and rob it of its
natural juiciness. Whatever your cooking method, keep the
temperature low to moderate.

If cuts are boneless, allow one-fourth to one-third pound
per serving; if bone in, estimate one-third to one-half pound
each; if very bony, three-fourths to one pound per serving.

Beef, veal, and lamb are graded by the USDA. Prime, the
top grade of these meats, often is unavailable in supermar-

kets. Choice, the next highest, is the most commonly sold grade, followed by Good. Standard and Commercial grades usually are not carried in stores. Meats are graded as a sign of expected eating quality. Grading is not required by law. Pork is not graded by the USDA as it does not have the variations of quality found in these other meats.

Beef. Meat to many means beef, and a variety of classic dishes using beef have come to us through the years. Beef Wellington, Beef Stroganoff, and Beef Fondue are three. The incomparable Chateaubriand is another classic beef dish.

From the most tender juicy steak to the common hamburger, beef is the basis for much of our American cooking. From pioneer days we have been a land where meat is plentiful. Although we like the meat-stretching dishes, often our beef is served as a steak or roast. Whatever dish we choose to cook, if it is delicious and attractively served, it is worthy company fare.

Fortunately for us, and especially to those married to "meat and potato men," there are many beef cuts that will provide appetizing, nutritious, and economical entrées. Knowledge of a wide variety of cuts is important to identifying good buys. A steer is not all sirloin steaks and rib roasts.

Leftover cooked beef is money in the refrigerator, so treat it with respect. The planned-over beef can come back in a variety of entrees from hot sandwiches to enchiladas, from salads to an appetizing pie, from casseroles to frozen TV dinners. Cooked beef, like other meats, freezes better when covered with a gravy.

Hamburger vs. Extra Lean Ground Beef. USDA researchers showed that one hundred patties each of hamburger and extra lean ground beef of identical weight still weighed the same after cooking. The extra lean patties had lost weight in water vapor, but the hamburger swam in its own fat. When we see the fat in the skillet, we conclude the meat has cooked away. We now know this isn't the deciding factor on which to base our choice between the two.

Except for the fat, hamburger and extra lean ground beef are nutritionally the same. Healthwise, this is an important difference. Our villians again—cholesterol and calories—must be dealt with, for they are killers in excess regardless of where we find them. If we choose to save the money and buy hamburger, we should blot the cooked pattie between paper towels before eating. If we brown hamburger meat for casseroles, we should pour it into a sieve after cooking to allow the excess fat to drain away. Pour off the fat and wipe the skillet with a paper towel before returning the browned hamburger to the skillet and adding other ingredients.

The fat in hamburger makes it more tender and juicy. Logically, one would assume that it would grill better. However, when dripping fat causes the charcoal to flame up and char any meat, that *charred portion only* is believed to be a carcinogen. In other words, it is believed to be a cause of cancer.

Either hamburger or extra lean ground beef is a good nutritious food. All meats should have fats drained off. No meat should be charred.

A good multipurpose hamburger mix can be made by frying chopped onions, garlic, and celery tops in a little fat. Add hamburger, stir, and cook until red disappears. Drain fat. Season with catsup, Worcestershire sauce, and salt and pepper, and simmer twenty minutes. Cool and refrigerate. Discard all solid fat. Package, label, and freeze. Four pounds of hamburger makes five pints of mix.

This mix may be heated and served on buns; used in a

casserole of noodles and mixed vegetables with cheese sprinkled on top, then baked until cheese melts; mixed with rice and used to stuff green peppers; used with sliced mushrooms, cream of mushroom soup, and sour cream as Stroganoff over noodles or rice; used as a spaghetti sauce with grated parmesan cheese; used for mock pizzas by spreading on lightly toasted English muffins, covered with cheese, sprinkled with oregano, and broiled until cheese is bubbly.

Pork. Prior to this century we raised hogs for lard. Today's hogs have been bred with 57 percent less fat than a few years ago and 22 percent more protein. This is significant for health reasons.

The marbling of fat in pork tissue makes it a tender, juicy meat ideal for grilling and all dry-cooking methods. When selecting pork, the lean should be firm and fine grained and should range in color from the grayish pink of fresh pork to the delicate rose of cured pork.

Because pork can be cooked with all the easy, dry heat methods as well as moist methods, it is a delight to prepare. A roast in the oven is virtually effortless. Pork grills and broils and fries. Stuffed or butterfly chops add variety for pork lovers. Pork is tasty in stir-fried and Oriental dishes, casseroles, stews, salads, and sandwiches.

Ham, one of the favorite pork products, is too big a cut for normal family meals unless you want to freeze leftovers in several ways. When you buy a ham, ask your butcher to cut it in halves or thirds. Freeze all but one portion. As you use ham, bits become treasures used in:

> ham salad
> julienne strips for chef salad
> omelets
> casseroles
> au gratin vegetables

cubes for appetizers
sliced thinly for sandwiches

A canned ham is a good emergency meat, but it must be refrigerated. Some may be frozen. For any type of ham, a glaze of barbecue sauce, mustard, or any traditional ham topping will add extra color and flavor.

Poultry. As a rule poultry is lower in calories, cholesterol, and cost than other meats while being high in protein and other nutrients, making it both a healthy and a wise purchase. It is lower in calories and cholesterol if cooked without the skin and not fried. Unless you are buying a boned breast or a boned, smoked bird it is economical.

Poultry is versatile, and almost everyone enjoys it. Every nationality has its poultry specialities. It's as casual as finger-lickin' fast food and as elegant as cordon bleu. It is also seasonless in its appeal.

Chicken recipes are endless, for this economical feast is favored by young and old. Many recipes, such as chicken pieces dipped in a mixture of sour cream and mustard, then rolled in seasoned crumbs and baked, are equally good hot or cold.

Large turkeys are often used at holiday times as a loss leader to get you into the store. That makes them an extraordinary bargain. Cut in half, the turkey can look classic for the feast meal, and the other half can be used later in preparing casseroles, salads, stir-fry with vegetables, sweet and sour for a Chinese meal, and hot and cold sandwiches just as chicken is used.

There are specialty birds available at a considerably higher price. Thanksgiving for one or two might not seem as lonely or overwhelming if two little Cornish hens were stuffed and colorfully garnished on a small platter.

Game. The wild duck, goose, pheasant, quail, grouse, etc., are game treats not readily available to most of us. If you do have access to them, by all means find a way to celebrate and share them with some special friends. This would also be true of rabbit, squirrel, venison, or any game. Good recipes are available.

The main difficulty in cooking is to counteract the often extreme dryness of the flesh, caused by an almost total lack of fat. One method used by many when using venison or other game is to wrap each thick cut with raw bacon before cooking. Or be liberal with the butter.

Fish and Shellfish. Women who fish or who are married to fishermen may have a good supply of either the real thing or stories of how the big one got away. Those of us who predate freezers will remember the teaching that you only ate seafood in months that had an *R* in their spelling. Since freezers and freezer transports are almost universally available, seafood is available year round, just as the tall tales have always been.

Fish and seafood are highly nutritious, and most varieties are very low in cholesterol and low in calories unless fried. Broiled or poached, fish are usually found on weight reduction and therapeutic diets.

Some of the seafood is very expensive. There are imitations at about half the cost made from lobster pieces, shrimp, and perhaps other seafoods. Nutritionally, the imitations won't harm you although they do contain artificial flavors and coloring. But they are not as nutritiously rich as the seafood they represent. You may wish to try these and make your own judgment.

Fish generally is inexpensive. Because the flesh is so tender and quickly cooked, prepreparation is not advisable. Keep in your freezer only what your family catches or regularly enjoys. Other fish can be purchased year round as needed.

It is a good idea to have a few cans of red salmon and tuna on your emergency shelf.

Cooking Methods

Because of the cost, many cooks feel insecure in preparing meats in a variety of ways. Therefore, we decided to include the following information from the National Live Stock and Meat Board.

There are means and appliances for preparing meats, but there are just two basic cookery methods. One method is by dry heat. The other is by moist heat. These encompass all ways, including roasting, broiling, panbroiling, panfrying or stirfrying, deep fat frying (all are dry heat); or, by braising and cooking in liquid (both are moist heat).

Dry heat is recommended for already tender cuts— steaks, chops, roasts, and burgers. Moist heat is the method recommended for cooking and tenderizing less tender cuts —such as pot-roasts, meat for stew and some steaks. Many cuts can be prepared by either dry or moist heat, providing variety.

Roasting

1. Place meat, fat side up, on rack in open roasting pan.
2. Insert meat thermometer so bulb is centered in roast.
3. Do not add water. Do not cover.
4. Roast in slow oven 350 F.°) to approximately 5 F. below desired doneness as indicated on meat thermometer.
5. Allow roast to stand for 15 to 20 minutes before carving. Temperature usually will rise about 5 F. during this time.

Broiling

1. Set oven regulator for broiling (preheat if desired) or start outdoor grill and wait until coals are covered with ash.

2. Place meat 3 to 5 inches from heat. For thinner beef cuts, 2 to 3 inches from heat.

3. Broil until meat is brown on one side.

4. Turn and broil second side until done.

5. Season each side after browning if desired.

Panbroiling

1. Place meat in heavy frying-pan. (Lightly grease pan for lean cuts.)

2. Do not add water. Do not cover.

3. Cook slowly, turning occasionally.

4. Pour fat from pan as it accumulates.

5. Brown meat on both sides.

6. Cook to desired doneness. Season as desired.

Panfrying

1. Brown meat on both sides in small amount of fat.

2. Season as desired.

3. Do not cover.

4. Cook at moderate temperature until done, turning occasionally.

Salads

Ah, salads! The sky is the limit when it comes to salads. Unfortunately, many of us get in a rut and prepare only one or two well-known salads and never explore the many choices available to us today.

Generally, salads provide fiber and many significant vitamins and minerals. We can expect them to be lower in calories than other dishes we serve. Salads are more popular

than ever because of our growing health and weight awareness.

Usually greens of some type are the basis for many salads.
There are many kinds of lettuce plus spinach, romaine,
parsley, endive, and cabbage. Also, many other leaves and
green vegetables (beet leaves, broccoli, raw peas) are a nutritious base. The choices of carrot strips, cucumbers,
tomatoes, celery, radishes, and onions are obvious. However, the addition of seeds or nuts, cheese tidbits, beet
slices, cauliflower, sprouts, egg slices, and meat, fish, or
poultry make the variety endless.

We discuss fruit salads in our "sweets" chapter. However,
these can be as a meal accompaniment as well as saved for
dessert. Then there is the whole realm of gelatin salads.
Some might be sweet and others quite tart. Foods such as
baked turkey or chicken go well with a sweet/sour gelatin
salad, perhaps red or green for certain holidays. We avoid
those popular gelatin salads which have a lot of sweet,
whipped topping blended into a sweet gelatin with little
other food of value. There simply are more nutritious things
to prepare and enjoy.

A salad can be the whole meal with the addition of an
appropriate bread and dessert. These salads are some we
like in that category:

Mexican salad (ground beef, tortilla chips, lettuce, onions, tomatoes, avocados, olives, cheddar cheese, kidney
beans, and whatever else you like plus dressing or sauce).
This is especially good with hot cheesy muffins. We like to
toss in the chips, lettuce, avocado, and tomatoes at the table
or just prior to eating as this salad tends to get soggy when
left over.

Stuffed tomato, avocado, or pineapple slice (use tuna salad, chicken salad, or whatever you enjoy).

Chef salad, with slivers of ham, cheese, and chicken or turkey plus many good cold and crisp vegetables.

Seafood or meat salad, such as crab, lobster, chicken, or turkey.

Fruit and cheese plate is especially delicious when the fruits are fresh. This goes well with warm blueberry or bran muffins.

Chicken or turkey salad. The recipes are plentiful for these two specialties . . . some with fruits (mandarin oranges, pineapple, white grapes), or nuts or water chestnuts.

Pasta salads, usually a bit tart and tossed with some leftover meat, poultry or cold cuts, green or ripe olives, and a host of other things such as pimento and green onions to add texture, flavor, and color. It can be made ahead, and it improves as it marinates in a light oil/vinegar dressing.

Often overlooked as the whole meal concept is the salad bar. You can really do your own thing here and with adequate protein (cheese, nuts, seeds, or slivers of meat) it is fun, filling, nourishing, delicious, and tailored entirely to individual tastes. Toasted garlic bread, muffins, or a variety of crackers are in order plus whatever dessert you choose.

For your salad bar you can try some new salad foods such as raw yellow squash, turnip, or zucchini slices. Many persons learn they like some vegetables better raw than cooked. Is this telling us that we tend to overcook most vegetables? You won't have to encourage family or guests to return for second servings. Have several dressings and oil and vinegar available.

For the most part we prefer to add the dressings individually at the table as tastes differ, unless, of course, the salad is supposed to marinate prior to serving. This solves the problem of wilted vegetables which cannot be retrieved in plastic bags for another time. Whether you make your own dressings or buy them, a variety is available. With oil, vinegar, and seasonings you never run out of a favorite.

Other salads which we like to accompany a meal include:

—Broccoli and cauliflower: add two parts of fresh broccoli pieces to one part cauliflower pieces, pimentos, ripe olives, garbanzo beans, water chestnuts, sweet onion slices, and fresh mushrooms. Give a light coating of Italian or oil/vinegar dressings. This needs to marinate several hours or overnight.

—Bean salad with at least three kinds of beans (green, waxed, kidney), plus onions, red bell pepper, and light marinade.

—Fresh spinach leaves, sweet onion rings, bacon bits, mandarin orange slices, and cashew nuts. Good with a sweet/sour or creamy celery seed dressing.

—Layered lettuce salad with a layer each of shredded lettuce, sliced hard-cooked eggs, bacon pieces, frozen peas, chopped onion and celery, shredded cheese, and sealed with a mayonnaise/sour cream topping. Chill overnight. This recipe has many variations.

—Middle East chopped tomato, onions, mint leaves, cucumbers, ripe olives, lemon juice, a bit of cooked rice or pasta, and olive oil and vinegar.

—Waldorf salad made of apples, celery, nuts, and grapes with mayonnaise.

—Slaw has become easier than ever with a food processor. Unless you can use the whole head at once, process it all but store about half the grated cabbage in an airtight container in the fridge before adding dressing and seasonings. It keeps several days that way.

—Grated carrots, crushed pineapple, and lemon gelatin. Of course, you always use the fruit juice for part of the hot liquid to dissolve the gelatin. Most gelatin salads are simple and, of course, can be made ahead and forgotten. Experiment with different vegetables and develop some new recipes for yourself.

—Tender asparagus on lettuce with tomato.

—Fully ripe avocado and tomato slices or quarters, with a touch of lemon, cracked black pepper, and oil/vinegar dressing.

Frozen fruit salads are still popular with certain meals but may be a bit high in calories for most of us. This also is true of a favorite "five-cup salad" using one cup each of mandarin orange slices, coconut, pineapple tidbits, sour cream, and chopped marshmallows.

Potato or pasta salad are perennial favorites for a cookout. They go with chicken, baked ham, or cold cuts and are generally liked by most people. With these as well as other salads, strive for variety in color, flavors, and textures, and use as many fresh ingredients as possible.

Convenience Foods and Mixes

If this were a cookbook, this one subject could take a volume all its own. The knowledge that there are endless recipes which can be matched with your desires and needs will at least put you on the right track to find them.

Convenience mixes sell in the simplest forms as self-rising flour or meal. Then more sophisticated are baking mixes with directions for making whatever you want to make from them. Instant puddings, cake, and brownie mixes, canned biscuits, boxed dinners, brown-and-serve cookies, and hundreds of products are partially prepared for convenience.

Homemade convenience foods have two great advantages over purchased ones. They are significantly cheaper, and they will contain only the ingredients you choose to put in them. The mix you make will surely be lower in sodium and additives you would not choose. This is important for those with health-related concerns of diabetes, hypertension, etc. You can also enrich your diet by replacing white flour with whole wheat, reducing sugar, adding bran, and adjusting the kinds and amounts of fat.

The varieties of mixes you can make yourself include:
corn bread mixes
whole wheat biscuit mixes
basic biscuit mixes
pudding and pie-filling mixes
sauce mixes
herb-stuffing cubes
seasoned rice mix
beef gravy base
chicken gravy base
Italian seasoning mix
Mexican seasoning mix
pastry mix
cookie mix
brownie mix
basic cake mix
beverage mix
multipurpose hamburger mix
all-purpose stew mix

It is an art to know which of these you would use creatively and in quantity enough to make them practical for you. No one has the storage or tastes for all these mixes, so being selective is the key.

There are cookbooks in your local library with these and

other mixes and your Extension Office will also be able to help you find the ones you need.

Potpourri

When you come right down to it, there is much more to enjoying family and friends than preparing meals for them. But if there is a mealtime included, there are ways of being together and sharing the work involved. Some of these shared meals can be memorable guest times or casual family fun.

It's always fun to grill. Guests or family can bring their own meat for your hot grill, or they simply can select a kabob, patty, chop, or steak from your tray and cook it the way they prefer. This would be easy on the hosts and enjoyable for the participants.

A planned or unplanned potluck type of meal which women especially like is a salad luncheon. Ask each guest to bring one salad and the hostess sets the tables and furnishes the bread and beverages.

Fondue can be an enjoyable meal where cooking your own is a part of the entertainment. With beef fondue all that's needed is a baked potato, green salad, and sauces for the meat and dessert. Cheese fondue is similarly easy. It takes the evening to eat dinner and the conversation is relaxed and easy.

Crepes make marvelous adult party fare, but older children also love "fixing their own." The batter should be made and refrigerated overnight. Cooking stations can be at the range and on the counter using hot plates. Filling and garnish choices can be made ahead. Both main-dish and dessert batters and fillings can be offered. Men get competitive about who cooks the best-looking crepe. Everyone loves it.

Doughnut fries and candy pulls are ideal participatory evenings if your waistline can stand the strain. Dessert parties also have become less popular as we have become more health conscious, but there are occasional times when we can indulge ourselves and our friends with these sweet treats.

Around the holidays, a cookie swap is beneficial and enjoyable to everyone. Each of twelve participants brings twelve packages of a dozen of her cookies to share, complete with duplicates of recipes. Best of all, she brings a plate of twelve cookies to give everyone a taste. Then each friend goes home with an assortment of twelve dozen homemade cookies for her family. It's much, much easier to bake three batches of the same recipe than it is to bake a variety of cookies, so this can be a time-saver too.

Progressive dinners are another typical holiday party style, for they give everyone a chance to visit three to five beautifully decorated homes. The dinner can be a block party where everyone walks house to house. If it requires a lot of driving, it's better to meet at the last house and car pool from there. You enjoy good company while driving, avoid parking problems, and your own car is convenient when the party's over. Progressive dinners are ideal in a senior citizen residence, condo, or apartment complex and can be held in any season.

Sometimes there are community events such as a Picnic at the Pops, where tables for eight must be reserved. Someone needs to take the initiative and organize a party to attend. That can be an unusual and a convenient way to entertain. Tailgating before the football game, stopping for pizza after church, or organizing a workday for a needy charity—include a sack of sandwiches and thermos of lemonade for those who help—are all fellowship times outside the home.

Almost any picnic is a casual potluck away from home. Being outside in the fresh air with some physical activity usually increases both hunger and thirst. It's a time when you don't have to be overly concerned about details, so once you've planned well, it is a "hang-loose-and-enjoy" kind of affair. If you use disposable paper products, be sure you buy them on sale; they can be costly.

Family reunions and celebrations are special to the people involved. Usually Mom is the "workhorse" of kids' birthday parties. But for parental anniversaries and family reunions, a good organizer will early on include others in the planning and work involved. Then everyone gets more out of it.

All of us have single friends whom we need to see occasionally. You may take them with you to the Decorator's Showcase or some special event; they'll love it, and afterward treat yourselves to whatever sounds good to you.

A pizza party is a lot of fun. With dough waiting in the pans, let each pair dress their own with sauce and all the "fixin's." (Your food processor will make all that slicing, chopping, and grating a breeze.) When a pizza is ready and others are baking, let the creators act as hosts, cutting and serving their own and keeping the beverages poured.

Salad, sandwich, baked potato, and taco bars are casual meals where all can participate. "Cincinnati chili" is big in our part of the country. It's a spicy, meaty chili on which you pile chopped onions, shredded cheese, red beans, and whatever you like. Some like it served over thin pasta. The sports and TV fans may raid the crockpot freely when it is full of the hot, tempting chili base.

Pancake and waffle suppers are easy and lend themselves

to several "master chefs." Along with sausage, bacon, or ham provide a variety of toppings such as berries, nuts, and syrups.

An ethnic party could include a prize for the most authentic or interesting costume, a prize for the most interesting information about the ethnic group, and a potluck (assigned by categories) of foods typical of the nation.

Whether you host a carol sing, sales party, bridal or baby shower, neighborhood association, or a church group, just your genuine welcome is a gift for each one who comes. Co-hosting makes it easier and is a good way to become comfortable entertaining guests.

One friend of ours had several young mothers over for lunch. Frances helped the moms feed the children in her kitchen. Then the hired baby-sitter took all the children to the park while the mothers enjoyed the luxury of a quiet, adult meal. What thoughtfulness!

For the employed woman, inviting a friend to meet her for lunch may be the ideal opportunity to see someone she enjoys. Even picking up deli sandwiches and drinks to enjoy together out under the trees in lovely weather may be a refreshing change from the clamor of the restaurant.

If you have a skill you've been asked to teach, tell the "students" to bring a sandwich, and you'll keep the tea kettle hot. A work session involving mothers of infants or young children also would be more productive with a sitter helping out.

In other chapters we have suggested ways of sharing with others—ways to say "I care." But nothing does it better than having a heart of compassion. That transcends all else.

11
Simple Sweets

Sugar and spice,
And everything nice,
That's what little girls are made of!

And "sugar and spice" is what big girls are supposed to serve guests—or so tradition dictates.

Meals often have been considered in the same way as speeches. If you could just finish with something memorable, then what went before wasn't so crucial. That erroneous notion has encouraged us to make desserts (1) oversweet, (2) overrich, (3) overtime-consuming, (4) overemphasized, and (5) oversized.

Add to that the fact that invariably the grand prize winner of a Gourmet Gala is an elaborate dessert. And most of us have twice as many dessert recipes as other kinds. So you see that promoting the idea of simple sweets is similar to swimming upstream. But we are willing to plunge in where angels fear to tread. Besides, we are suggesting that easy entertaining could involve serving dessert only, especially for the host in a nonmeal situation.

Some persons seldom eat dessert (for example, Marge's son, Jim), but others don't feel finished without something to satisfy their sweet tooth. Most of us with our new health awareness fit somewhere in between. We opt for self-discipline in small servings rather than never enjoying desserts at all, realizing that rich, sweet desserts nullify our good intentions of eating fewer empty calories.

As we wrestle to tame our food passions, we are also striving for less complicated food preparation. Consider, then, some sweets/desserts which fit within the time and nutritional boundaries we have set for ourselves.

Fruit
- Fresh fruit, with or without cheeses.
- Spiced canned fruit compote, warm or cold.
- Fruit cobbler "my way" (less sugar and more fruit).
- Fruit salads (fresh or a combination of fresh, canned, and frozen).
- A baked apple served warm with or without sauce.
- Dried fruit, cooked or not.
- Flaming fresh pineapple for an exotic touch.

Some specific fruits might include:

Melons
- Watermelon is a treat in its own class.
- Melon balls (a good recipe includes equal amounts of cantaloupe and honeydew balls, a bit of frozen orange concentrate—all well chilled).
- Honeydew balls and fresh blueberries or other combinations topped with coconut.

Berries
- Strawberries are good any way . . . from whole, topped with a sprinkle of powdered sugar, to old-fashioned shortcake and whipped cream.
- Any berries, fresh or frozen.

Citrus
- Fresh orange slices or sections sprinkled with coconut.
- Grapefruit and orange sections.
- Juices frozen into homemade Popsicles.
- Frozen orange juice concentrate or apricot nectar thickened with cornstarch and served warm over vanilla ice cream or plain cake.

Although it's hard to improve on fruit for the finale to any meal, we all occasionally want something different. We recommend:

Hot Bread
- Hot bread, butter, and jam (quick breads such as muffins, corn bread, biscuits, fruit/nut loaf, or yeast breads in endless variations).

Custards, Puddings, Gelatins, Yogurts, and Mousses
- Fruit and flavored gelatin.
- Yogurt mixed with fresh fruit, nuts.
- Pudding topped with nuts and whipped cream.
- Baked custards, warm or chilled, served plain or with coconut or chopped nuts.
- Mousse—prepared the day ahead.

Ice cream and sherbets
- Topped with fresh fruit, cooked toppings, sauces, or served plain.
- Made into banana splits or pie or cake a la mode.
- Shaped into balls, then rolled in coconut, chopped nuts, or granola and served as is or with warm topping.
- Homemade ice cream—fantastic!

Cakes

Cakes have captivated many cooks because they can be made ahead. Many mixes defy all but the most perceptive connoisseur. Some cakes that we especially like are:

- Pineapple upside-down cake, baked in an oven-proof skillet and ready to eat warm from the oven . . . no additional topping needed.
- Angel cake, with or without icing, served with fresh berries.
- Homemade carrot cake, full of nuts, pineapple, raisins, and grated carrots. Who says this isn't nutritious?

Cheesecake

Ah, yes, the jewel among cakes is the cheesecake. We enjoy a sour cream topping and perhaps fresh berries on each serving.

Bar cookies

- Brownies, or lemon, prune, and date bars are easily served and travel well if need be.

Pancakes, waffles, crepes

Griddle cakes can be desserts or served as the main course. They are delectable company cuisine.

If for dessert, plan a lighter main course such as soup or salad; then serve

- Fruit pancakes or waffles with fruit on top.
- Chocolate waffles with nuts and whipped cream.
- Crepes with fruit fillings and toppings.

Pastries

You don't need any prodding to think of your favorite pie. We consider a fresh apple pie, warm from the oven and served with cheddar cheese, suitable for the most discriminating palate. It is wise to serve pies when the main course is light or when guests are invited for dessert only.

Shape several pie shells at one time and freeze. Then you can have warm pie (or quiche) in little time. Master a few fillings and when appropriate to the recipe, experiment with using less sugar and butter. You may find that you prefer it that way. We were pleased to see a book recently in which the author included many traditional desserts made with sugar substitutes and less fat. This is but one of many today which feature calorie control, so "less is better" is catching on.

For the most part the sweets we've listed make sense for today's life-styles. Much, much more could be written, for dessert possibilities are almost limitless. Sometimes nuts or mints or just a dessert coffee are most appropriate. Your own tastes, your guests, the time available, and the rest of your menu will dictate your dessert decisions.

Dessert recipes abound, so get out all those cookbooks or check almost any magazine and mark a few new confections to try. Someone will be asking you to share your secrets before you can say, "Yield not to temptation"!

12
Heavy Facts
(For Enlightened People)

All of us have known many overweight persons. We've seen the misery that overwhelms some and the seeming indifference of others.

We know young mothers who have struggled for years to lose the excess gained during pregnancy. We know men who wouldn't abuse their bodies with drugs or alcohol, yet overeat until they are cheating their families of years of togetherness.

All of us have loved ones who pay the staggering price of poorer health. But that is not the only price. Overweight people miss so much socially because of their fragile self-images. Often they hesitate to entertain, and deep relationships are avoided. Uppermost is the bruising penalty exacted by a rejecting society which is obsessed by physical appearance.

It is ironical that while so much of the world starves, we are killing ourselves with our abundance. First Corinthians 6:19-20 is one Bible passage which urges us to honor our bodies as temples of the Holy Spirit. Any excess is harmful and a poor testimony to the power of God in our lives. Only by claiming His help can we become victors.

We started simply to suggest a few low-calorie recipes and ideas for entertaining when weight is a concern. But we decided that would be superficial. Reading about low-calorie food is not enough; we must delve deeper.

Hopefully the facts below will be usable if you need them. If not, pray for those still struggling!

When You Entertain, Here's How to Maintain Your Weight and Nutritional Balance and to Help Your Guests to Do the Same—Be Aware That:

1. Entertaining directly relates to weight control.
- Many guests watch their calorie consumption, so offer a choice (fruit in place of pastry) or small servings.
- Many overweight people hesitate to entertain because of their own dietary needs, or they think everything must be rich or elaborate for guests.
- Others give up trying to be trim because of a lifestyle which includes eating out or cooking for guests.
- The thoughtful hostess doesn't insist on seconds or otherwise cause others to "fall off the wagon."

2. Overweight is the penalty for overeating.
- Food Intake = Energy Used + Fat Stored.
- For each pound you are overweight, you have overeaten 3500 calories.

3. Excuses for overweight are usually cop-outs.
- "It's my glands" (not one in a hundred).
- "All my family were fat" (and they also overate).
- "I hardly eat anything" (but all the wrong stuff).
- "I never eat breakfast" (but I make up for it later).
- "I don't eat as much as I used to" (but I use less energy too).

- "My family likes me pleasingly plump" (be honest).

4. For whom is weight control important?
- Babies/children—there is no such thing as "baby fat." Once a fat cell forms, it is there for life. Even if persons lose weight, the empty cell is waiting to refill very quickly.
- Adolescents—self-image and peer acceptance are closely associated with appearance. Vitality is essential.
- Adults—career advancement, good health, vitality and personal relationships are often tied to one's weight.
- Older adults—too many pounds promote diabetes, heart disease, high blood pressure, arthritis, stroke, back and foot problems, gallstones, and kidney diseases as well as fatigue, less attractive looks, and shortened life.

5. How do you know what your weight should be?
- Your ideal weight as a young adult is your ideal weight for life.

6. What should you do to lose weight?
- Decide you need to and are going to lose weight.
- To lose *1 pound a week, eat 500 fewer calories* than you need every day. (This could equal *52 pounds a year loss*.)
- Never go on a diet under 1200 calories unless you are being supervised by your doctor. At 1200 calories and above, you can eat a balanced diet.
- Use the basic food groups from USDA. Choose the low-calorie foods in each group. Eat recommended

portions only. Avoid fat and sugar. You will be eating 1200 calories, approximately.
- Don't skip any meals and eat a balanced diet.
- Plan your snacks as a part of your total food intake.
- Eat measured servings, no seconds.
- Eat foods with adequate fiber and starch.
- Eliminate as much sugar, salt, and fat as possible.

7. Why do diets fail 80 percent of the time?
- They do not change lifetime habits.
- They often cannot be maintained for long periods because of cost or nutrient deficiencies.
- They often require preparing two menus every meal.

8. What exercises are best?
- Walk rapidly past closed refrigerator.
- After eating allotted food, place both hands on the table and push!
- Shake head vigorously from side to side when offered snacks or second helpings.
- Do whatever exercise you enjoy enough to do regularly.

Use Your Head to Help Your Body

9. What is a calorie?
- A calorie is the measure of energy in food.
- There are: 4 calories in a gram of protein, starches, and sugar.
  9 calories in a gram of fat.

- There are 28 grams in an ounce; that's 453 grams in a pound.

10. How can I figure how many calories I need?

- If you are: Passive   Moderately Active   Active
  Man's Desired Wt. X 16,   21,   or   26
  Woman's " " X 14,   18,   or   22
- For each decade in age past 25, subtract 50.
- This will give you the calories you need per day.
- For example:

  Female wants to weigh 130 and is passive:
    130 X 14 = 1820 calories.

  If she is 55 years old, 1820 − 150 = 1670 calories. If she eats 1670 calories a day, her weight slowly will drop to 130 pounds and stay there.

Practical Suggestions for Hosts or Guests to Control Weight

Do Buy:
- Only healthful foods—a lot of fresh foods.
- Low-calorie foods instead of high-calorie foods.
- Bulky, watery, crispy foods; not greasy, gooey, sweet foods.
- When eating out, order unembellished foods, fruits, low-calorie dressings, broiled meat, and fish.

Do Serve:
- Exact amounts of foods—measure for a while.
- Tested recipes to avoid tasting when cooking.

- Food with herbs, spices, lemon juice, etc., for seasoning.
- Plates garnished with raw carrots, berries, or an orange slice.
- An abundance of cold water or juices, always available to help the serious dieter or guests.
- Or keep "help yourself" low-calorie snacks in fridge.

Whether You Are the Host or a Guest, Do:
- Eat portion sizes you need—no seconds.
- Eat three meals a day, planned from basic food groups.
- Drink 6-8 glasses of water daily.
- Cut food into small bites and eat very slowly.
- Rest your fork on your plate between bites.
- Use a salad plate or smaller plate.
- Remember your entire food intake must be counted, such as snacks, drinks, and toppings.
- Eat or drink only what you have decided to at a party.

And Remember, Do:
- Store food out of sight; put away leftovers before eating.
- Begin trimming down as soon as you recognize you weigh too much. Don't wait!
- Give yourself time to lose. You didn't gain it in a month, and you won't lose it that soon.
- Learn to judge serving size. Decide at once how much you are going to leave on the plate or in the dish.
- Exercise moderately several times a day.

- Develop interests that don't involve food.
- Post a "before" picture on the fridge door.
- Reread these fact sheets daily.
- Lose weight for those you love if not for yourself.

13
When Things Go Wrong

If you've never had anything go wrong, you aren't even breathing, much less doing any entertaining. With our combined seventy-five years of entertaining we have:

been rained on and rained out

had power failures

been stood up

had guests come on the wrong day

turned up the wrong day ourselves

had guests come for dinner instead of for tea

served meals hours late

prepared what guests cannot eat

had incompatible guests

had a variety of food flops

had half a crowd or twice the expected number

and you name it, we've done it.

The amazing thing is that it never cost us a relationship; we have trouble even remembering all the circumstances, and a hundred years from now no one will ever know the difference.

Some of the big goofs are hilarious in retrospect, and many of Jean's were related to cultural differences overseas. There was the time the neighbors reluctantly cooked a peacock sent ahead by the Pakistani Thanksgiving guest, only to discover the honored guest had sent it as a pet for the host's children!

Or in America, Jean melted chocolate bits and carefully lined fluted cupcake papers with it to form dainty chocolate cups to hold orange sherbet. When guests cut through the cold, brittle chocolate, pieces shot across the table in every direction.

What can you do when this happens? Running to the bedroom to cry isn't the answer; nor is moving out of town so you never have to see these folks again. If you have a sense of humor, this is its golden hour. If you can't manage a good laugh, at least try a quick apology and observe that you, like Edison, have found one more thing that won't work.

The weather repeatedly has been the reason things seemingly went wrong. Marge had invited four guests for a patio dinner at seven (lasagna, salad bar, Italian bread sticks, iced tea, fruit and cheese, and coffee).

Suddenly an electrical storm shattered the stillness of the late summer afternoon. All power in that area of town was shut off.

"This won't last long," Marge told herself, trying to remain composed and making sure that everything was ready for that moment when the electricity reappeared. Just to feel secure, she put two large cans of red salmon from the emergency shelf into the freezer where they could chill. (She knew it was verboten to open the freezer when the power was off, but . . .)

The guests arrived promptly at seven. By 9:00 PM they had finished a light, intimate candlelight dinner in the dining room. You guessed it—they ate chilled red salmon with lemon wedges, salad, bread sticks, fruit and cheese, and iced tea. Both couples have since reminded Marge of that quiet, relaxing evening. One of the couples was grieving the recent loss of a son. Thus the changed setting really met their needs in a much better way than had been planned. The next morning at church, Marge was able to ask some newcomers home for dinner for hot lasagna, relishes/pickles, and sherbet. That meal was special because new friends were made that day.

If discretion is supposed to be the better part of valor, sometimes caution may be the major force in postponing dinner guests when the weather news is deplorable. We recently postponed a dinner scheduled in less than twenty-four hours because of dangerous snow and ice storms. Invited guests may hesitate to take the initiative, but the hosts should think of the safety and peace of their friends or family. Sure, we had cabin fever and really needed those friends. But consideration for others takes precedence.

Often the host and hostess have to help each other or guests "save face" or lessen embarrassment in certain situations. Jesus did this for the wedding host when He performed that first miracle at Cana. He surely would have us show thoughtfulness anytime we can.

Recently, our two families invited four mutual friends to dinner. The two of us had shared in planning the menu and preparing the food. But we hadn't discussed the serving aspect. Working closely together for years can result in taking things for granted.

Everything went smoothly until the beginning of dessert. Guests were served ice cream in exquisite lotus-shaped bowls. The two warm toppings, in pitchers, were placed on a single tray and passed. Without a warning, the warm fudge sauce catapulted off the tray onto the lap of one guest and then onto the carpet.

"Sit still," host hubby said as he rose to get a wet cloth to soak some of the mess before it spread. "It's OK, Karen. I can get the stain out of your dress," countered the hostess. Confusion, frustration, a clothes change, and quick dress soaking followed. Then laughter! "What chapter is this in?" asked the victim, wrapped in a robe belonging to the hostess. "Chapter 13," we replied!

Later, when we analyzed what went wrong, we realized that we had neglected to discuss serving dessert. We should have either passed the sauces separately or set up a small dessert buffet where guests could top their ice cream. Planning can avert most human-error catastrophes.

If there is something unsanitary or unhealthy about a food or for any reason it cannot be eaten, simply remove it and go ahead. The less said, the better.

How do you handle it when you prepare a meal for a group and perhaps only half show up? People do forget, or their message may fail to reach you. It requires much grace to go on cheerfully. But the others of you can have an enjoyable evening. Or the opposite can happen, and twice as many arrive than you expected . . . they just happen in.

If there isn't enough food you can quickly stretch the meal by:

Adding an appetizer:
    fruit or vegetable juice
    cheese or dips with crackers
    package or canned soups

Stretching the main course with:
    applesauce or cranberry sauce
    pickles, relishes, or pickled beets
    adding another canned/frozen vegetable
    canned or spiced hot fruit
    adding bread—hot if possible—with butter and jam

And for dessert:

arrange a bowl of fresh fruit

cut smaller pieces of dessert and add a topping

frozen or canned fruit can stretch fresh fruit or top ice cream

or retrieve your stash of candy for that little taste of sweet

If we are inviting someone of a different nationality or religion for the first time, it may be advisable to ask whether there is any food they do not eat. For instance, Muslems don't eat pork, and Hindus are typically vegetarians. If you can't check ahead with them, it helps to provide a variety, including some foods which are plain or simple.

There may also be those among our closer friends who refrain from eating a food for medical or personal reasons. One rainy day when Marge had a large pot of homemade vegetable soup on the back burner, she asked a couple home from church for lunch. One of the guests is a vegetarian and would not have accepted the invitation had he known that the soup was full of meat too. She was glad Sam felt free to ask whether she had some cheese or peanut butter. She did, plus several other things were in the fridge which he ate with pleasure, and everyone enjoyed the meal.

This is a chance you take in your effort to expand your circle of friendships and with impromptu invitations. We've found that most people can eat scrambled eggs if they simply can't eat what you have, and we've even asked them to scramble their own—their way. Most of all, they will remember that you cared and did not become all unglued because they have different preferences.

Cultural habits may occasionally surprise us, too. Jean tells of another time in East Africa when her guests were a Masai couple who had never eaten in a house before. The lady threw her hot tea on the woolen carpet before being served a refill. The Lord gave grace in that situation and always will if we but ask.

Sometimes we plan too close for comfort when it involves travel or other uncontrollable situations. For example, planes are late. Perhaps one of the hosts is held up at work (for example, the busy doctor) and will be a couple of hours late. It isn't always possible to get to a phone or get the line when the unexpected happens. Those present should go ahead and eat. The latecomers feel less guilt, and the others will eat the food at its best.

There can always be an accident and a trip to the emergency room which takes hours. Unless appetites are ruined, the remaining persons should go ahead and eat. We've both been through this and feel that each situation is unique. Be guided by your own common sense, maturity, and the leading of the Lord.

The time Marge experienced this was when she was a guest for a large buffet dinner. Several people were helping the hostess. Suddenly the host suffered a heart attack, and the hostess rushed with him to the hospital. At the request of the hosts, the guests continued with the meal. Afterward everyone helped with the cleanup with a minimum of confusion or anxiety. We're glad to report that Jack recovered.

We recall many times that things went wrong simply because some food just flopped: the cake fell, the soup curdled, the bread burned, the pie refused to come out of the pan, or the oven smoked unmercifully because of a spill until it drove everyone outdoors. No one minds tears in their eyes if there is laughter on their lips, so as we've said, a sense of humor greatly helps.

Sometimes we can do as Jean's aunt did—fifty years ago— fill in the fallen cake with lots of fudge icing and make a memory. Or we've crumbled cake into a bowl of whipped cream and berries and changed the dessert (a type of unplanned English trifle). Switching foods at the last minute often happens, and nobody need know it. Or saying "I goofed and burned the beans, so we will have peas instead" may be needed when the disaster is obvious.

The trait we need to cultivate is to learn not to panic. It isn't the end of the world. How we handle the crisis is the key to how our guests and family feel. Usually there is enough food if there is enough grace on our part.

Admittedly, it isn't easy to remain in control when things go wrong, but perhaps an outer calm will soothe the others. One friend opened her home for days to the homeless needing food and shelter when a tornado almost destroyed their small community. Betty's compassion and self-control helped those who were shaken by their losses.

Jean tells of the time overseas when she was preparing homemade doughnuts for a visiting medical group. Abruptly the joy was overshadowed by a nearby bus wreck. Every able-bodied person was then pressed into unbelievable service for many hours. By the time the situation had stabilized, those who could get away then had that long-awaited hot coffee and doughnuts (cool by now) as they almost dropped from fatigue, shock, and hunger.

Anytime, anywhere, we might have to utilize every resource available to meet a particular need. Thankfully, most challenges will be minor. When a cake falls, let's keep it in perspective. The meal will be acceptable regardless, and our guests will appreciate the fact that we are as human as they!

Epilogue

So here we are—humans prone to make mistakes, striving to meet the demands on us, wrestling with our own particular problems, and really wanting to cherish and be cherished by the people in our lives. It is almost as if we are adding one more stress to think of the investment in time and effort it will take to be available and hospitable to them.

Throughout this book we have presented ways to make entertaining more possible and more enjoyable. As we have turned to the Bible as a practical guide for living, we find that both meeting physical needs, as Martha did, and enjoying a rich fellowship in the presence of Jesus, as Mary did, are desirable for harmony and balance. Either without the other would be incomplete.

This precious truth assumes that we know the One who makes things right, and that His motives are also ours. Making our hearts right and making everything work for good is something only God can do. All we have to do is ask.

Each of us has some of both Mary and Martha in us, and each of us will probably need to fine-tune our personalities, skills, and habits if we are to be able to say with enthusiasm, "Come and share our lives."